Norwell,

ROHALLION

BOOKS BY

DOUGLAS SUTHERLAND

Burgess and Maclean
The Yellow Earl
Against the Wind
The Landowners
Behold! The Hebrides
Tried and Valiant
Strike: a novel
Rohallion

ROHALLION

*Wild Life in
a Scottish home*

By
DOUGLAS SUTHERLAND

Illustrated by
CHARLES SUTHERLAND

HEINEMANN : LONDON

William Heinemann Ltd
15 Queen Street, Mayfair, London W1X 8BE

LONDON MELBOURNE TORONTO
JOHANNESBURG AUCKLAND

First published 1978

© DOUGLAS SUTHERLAND 1978

SBN 434 75203 7

For Jo-Jo

Printed and bound in Great Britain by
Morrison and Gibb Ltd, London and Edinburgh

1

WE SAT, Diana and I, huddled round the fire in the sitting room of our neo-Georgian box of a house in the middle of Buckinghamshire and gloomed.

Outside the rain was coming down in stair-rods turning the heavy clay soil into a glutinous morass which sucked off our Wellington boots if we ventured into the garden and the tinsel decorations of a Christmas just passed were still piled depressingly in the uncollected rubbish bins.

Soon it would be time to pick up the children from school. Normally they would have walked the mile and a half home but today the weather made it impossible. It was usually my job to fetch them but this time Diana volunteered.

"Anything is better," she said, "than sitting in this beastly house."

That set me off thinking.

We had bought the house a year before for all the right reasons.

The family were starting to grow up and it was time we settled somewhere. We wanted to be in the country but near enough to London for me to keep in touch with publishers and agents and all the other people upon whom my living depended. We had many good friends who lived nearby and the harsh croaking of the property speculators still had to make itself heard in that part of the land.

Somehow it had not worked out although it was not until that wet January afternoon that I really faced up to it.

In the first enthusiasm of ownership we had worked hard, papering and painting the inside of the house and hacking furiously at the undergrowth outside to try and restore the neglected garden to some semblance of order, but it had not been a rewarding task. The newly sown lawn persisted in looking as if it had a bad attack of eczema, the paper in the bedrooms drooped sadly from the damp walls whenever it rained and in the rare hot spells the sweet-sour smell of silage from the next door farm hung about everything with the persistence of mustard gas.

Even my yellow labrador, Mist, deprived of her regular days out shooting, sought to relieve her boredom by knocking old ladies off their bicycles as they made their innocent way past our garden gate.

Most serious of all the house was too small. We had our own two children living there, Diana's son by her first marriage and a young Scots nanny. But we both had other children by previous marriages and, with only three bedrooms, we could never have them to stay. We had talked of building on but without much enthusiasm. Instead we worried and fretted, unwilling to admit that we had been wrong to take the house in the first place.

I should have known that Diana was getting to the end of her tether when one morning I went through to the open-plan kitchen-diningroom which also served as a television room and a rumpus room for the children, to hear her say to them with a note of desperation in her voice. "Listen, why don't you three just go and play in the nice warm rain!"

That afternoon when she brought the children home from school and while she was still shaking the water off their anoraks in the hall I told her that I had decided we would have to move. In our household I am not accustomed to making unilateral decisions but this time I was sure that it was what Diana wanted as well. I was right.

After the children had gone to bed we spent a long time indulging the luxury of discussing where we would go. There was one small cloud of doubt at the back of our minds. Would anyone want to buy the horrid little house we had bought so impetuously and in which our small amount of capital was tied up?

If anything was needed to steel our resolve it came in the form of a letter from Diana's ex-husband. After his remarriage it had been agreed that he should take their daughter to live with him in Malta in the belief that there were excellent schools there and that the warm climate would do her good.

Now he wrote to say that it was not so. She was falling behind with her work at the Convent School, due largely to language difficulties and her pale complexion did not take kindly to the sun. Could we, after all, have her to live with us? We were overjoyed but it made the question of moving no longer a matter of speculation but of necessity.

It so happened that Diana and I had planned a trip to Scotland the following week, leaving the kids in the charge of the nanny.

Although I have spent much of my life wandering, I am Scottish by birth and upbringing, having spent my childhood in the Orkney Isles (See "Against the Wind" – Heinemann). My mother and brothers now lived in Perthshire and we frequently went there to visit them.

Mothers are the same the world over. When we told her that we had decided upon a move she said at once, "Of course you will be coming up to Scotland." Apart from her strong maternal instincts she is chauvinistically Scottish and cannot imagine anyone wanting to live anywhere else. That I should have left my homeland to earn a living she regarded at best as eccentric and at worst an act of treachery.

In fact a return to Scotland was one of the things which had never crossed our minds. In the week which had followed the arrival of the letter from Malta we had discussed many places as far apart as the Algarve and Andorra, the South Coast and the Lake District where we had spent a happy year writing a book but somehow Scotland had never come into our reckonings. Now I cannot think why but decisions of this sort have a habit of making themselves for you if you dither long enough.

One evening we were asked out for drinks by Archie Rose and his wife who live nearby – that is fifteen miles away which constitutes next door neighbourliness in Scotland.

Archie would have made a good abbot in the days before the dissolution of the monasteries. He is a bon vivant with a love of life and the dispenser of hospitality to saints and sinners alike. As it is he is well suited to his role as the senior partner in a distinguished firm of solicitors and accustomed to listen to the temporal troubles of others.

Most of the conversation that evening revolved around our problems of finding somewhere to live.

"Why don't you try and find somewhere up here?" he suggested, echoing the words of my mother.

"I want plenty of room," said Diana.

"And it must be cheap," I said.

"Lovely scenery," Diana enthused, "but not too far from shops and things."

"With perhaps some fishing of its own," I added, just to make the problem more difficult.

"I think I know just the place," said Archie.

Which was how we first came to hear of Rohallion.

2

THE DAY after our visit to Archie Rose was a Sunday and it was impossible to get in touch with anyone about getting permission to view the house.

Just the same we thought we would drive there and have a look at the outside. Archie's description had fired our imagination and we could not wait to go and view it for ourselves.

The driveway which leads to Rohallion opens off the A.9 which is the main road from Perth to Inverness and up and down which heavily loaded lorries grind their way in constant procession. I had driven up the road many times without noticing the unobtrusive white gates and that morning I only found them with difficulty.

It was a dull, cold day. Wisps of fog hung about the tops of the tall avenue of oaks and patches of snow still survived on the grass verges from the last fall of a week before. The avenue itself was rutted and potholed, sorely trying the springs of our ancient Rover.

"It reminds me of the opening shot of a bad French film," said Diana despondently. It was certainly not what we had expected.

The avenue is about three quarters of a mile long and we were just beginning to wonder if we were on the right track when the house loomed up suddenly ahead of us. A moment later and we came out of the trees and pulled up on a broad sweep of gravel outside the front door.

Immediately we got out of the car our unease disappeared. Here surely was the perfect setting for a house. Right in front of us, not twenty yards from the west side, we looked down on a small loch almost completely surrounded by bank upon bank of rhododendrons. On the further side of the water the ground rose steeply to a high pine clad ridge. A broad grassy terrace stretched along the loch side of the house whilst in front there were open lawns, interspersed with rose beds and in the centre, a rough timbered summer house over which honeysuckle climbed. There were rhododendrons and azaleas everywhere and towering above them massive trees of many different varieties.

It was obvious, in spite of the general impression of wildness, that, perhaps a century before, someone had planned the setting with great care. There were tall Cypresses, Wellingtonias and a majestic Douglas fir almost two hundred feet tall. There were cedars and walnuts and even great monkey puzzle trees all placed where they could be seen to their best advantage.

Perhaps the most surprising of all in the middle of the lawn there was a gnarled old Arboreum rhododendron which in mid January had already broken into a profusion of scarlet blooms.

When we turned our attention to the house, however, the evidence that some master planner had been at work at once disappeared. It was altogether an extraordinary creation. It might have been the result of a committee of architects each trying to impose his own style. The central feature was a great circular 70 foot tower round the base of which was clustered a Victorian exuberance of balconied rooms, and lesser spires and turrets.

We peered through the dusty front window panes, trying without much success to penetrate the gloom within. Then we took a walk to explore the back quarters. A stone archway gave access to an open courtyard overlooked by the windows of what were obviously the kitchens and the old servants rooms. They were heavily barred as was the custom of the early Victorians, anxious to prevent amorous housemaids from slipping out at night to keep assignations with grooms and gardener's boys.

As we entered the courtyard there was a flurry of wings as a flock of tame pigeons circled our heads before landing at our feet, cooing and strutting and cocking up their heads, obviously expecting to be fed.

We had come unequipped for such an eventuality so we could only look at them apologetically, shaking our heads and, absurdly, patting our pockets to show that they were really empty of corn or crusts of bread.

It was whilst we were behaving in this quite idiotic manner that a stocky tweed clad figure came round the corner of the house escorted by twenty or thirty Muscovy ducks, waddling along as fast as their short legs would permit and sometimes taking off in brief awkward flight in their efforts to keep up.

It occurred to me now with some embarrassment that we had no right to be poking around somebody else's property without permission. Conscious that the newcomer was looking at us with some suspicion I muttered something about being interested in taking the house. At once he gave us a friendly smile.

"Aye," he said, "it's about time somebody came to live here. These old places don't bear not living in ye ken." Then he added seriously, "I hope if you do come that you'll take over the burrds."

This was our introduction to Jimmy Wemyss, a keeper who lived three quarters of a mile further up the hill and was Rohallion's nearest neighbour. A moment later his wife joined us and together we walked back up the terrace whilst Jimmy threw out handfuls of grain to our importunate escort.

"That's what they call Buffalo Park," he told us, pointing to the high ground behind the house.

"A strange name. I wonder how it came to be called that."

"Because," said Jimmy, with devastating logic, "that's where they used to keep the buffalo." Then changing the subject he said, "Queen Victoria came here once. Said it was one of the most beautiful places she'd seen in Scotland."

Putting these fascinating snippets of information at the back of my mind to return to later, I asked if there were any trout in the loch.

"Teeming with them," said Jimmy. "The last folk never bothered with them. They were all for horses. Horse daft you know but decent enough people for all that," he added charitably. People who preferred riding horses to catching fish obviously puzzled Jimmy.

Mrs. Wemyss and Diana by this time were deeply engrossed in a discussion about such things so near to the female heart as delivery vans, hairdressers, laundries and schools, so Jimmy and I left them to it and wandered across the lawns towards the big Douglas fir which stood at the bottom end of the loch.

On the way, half hidden in the rhododendrons, we came across a slate-roofed boat house which housed a large flat-bottomed boat rather after the style of an English punt.

7

Jimmy gave it an appreciative kick. "Fine boat that was in its day and there's life in her yet. Over fifty years old she is. The lady who used to live here bought her in Gamages just after the Great War."

"Gamages?" I said. "That's an odd place to go for a boat."

"Bought everything at Gamages she did. She always wrote to them on Fridays and the things she ordered would arrive at Dunkeld station the following Tuesday. You got service in those days. Not like today."

We could have talked for a long time but it was getting dark early and the mist was coming down in earnest.

As we drove down the avenue Diana, who had been uncharacteristically quiet, said quite suddenly.

"Well that's settled then. We'll take the place."

I looked at her in astonishment.

"Look here. We haven't even discussed it yet and we don't know what it is likely to cost. Archie never told us it was a mini-castle. Besides it may be riddled with dry rot or anything."

But Diana had made up her mind and so, in spite of my protests, had I.

We borrowed the keys of the house two days after our unofficial visit and had a happy time exploring the interior. We climbed the sixty steps of the circular staircase which led to the top bedroom in the tower, admired the ornate wooden ceilings and looked with foreboding at the ancient Esse stove in the big kitchen.

To be absolutely truthful our enthusiasm would have been greater if I had not thought to take my mother with us. She lives in a perpetual state of apprehension that we are on the point of doing something quite dreadful and in consequence regards it as part of her maternal function to look on the gloomy side of things.

She started her campaign as we drove up the drive. By chance there had been two days of heavy rain and the great potholes were filled to overflowing. As we splashed our way through the flooding she gave it as her opinion that with another day of rain it would be quite impassable.

"I could always let the fishing," I remarked, determined to remain cheerful.

Once inside the house she had a real field day. The difficulty of furnishing such large rooms, the impossibility of keeping a house of fifteen rooms warm and still remaining solvent, and the probability that the whole place was overrun with rats, all got an airing as we made our tour.

Finally we came to a beautiful large bedroom, bright and sunny, with a high ceiling and tall windows opening onto a small Italianate balcony.

"We'll keep this room for you when you come and stay," I told her, placatingly.

"I wouldn't stay in this room if you offered me a thousand pounds," she declared.

"Why ever not?" said Diana. "I think it's a lovely room."

"Ghosts!" said my mother, her eyes rolling in her head like a mad dervish. "This room is haunted. I knew it the moment I came through the door."

It was not until we got home that she relented. Then seeing that we were determined to take the house whatever happened she forgot all her objections and we spent the rest of the evening in excited discussions of just what we would do if we managed to get it.

The weeks which followed were miserable ones.

Rohallion was part of the Murthly Estate which belongs to the Steuart-Fotheringham family, one of Perthshire's largest landowners. Even if we could have afforded it they would not sell, but they were prepared to let it on a long lease. They had a number of applicants and we would have to wait until they had all been considered.

We had both set our hearts on getting the house and talked of little else, but as the days passed by and we heard nothing we became almost convinced that our application had not been successful.

At the same time we had decided that come what may we would sell our little Buckinghamshire box and take a chance on finding somewhere else if Rohallion fell through. It was before the time of the great property boom and we soon discovered that the process of buying the house had been much simpler than the business of disposing of it.

It was not that there was any lack of interest. Particularly if it was a fine weekend we could be sure of a regular stream of visitors, eager-eyed and clutching their orders to view.

At first Diana and I gave them the red carpet treatment,

plying them with cups of coffee and talking knowledgeably about septic tanks, heating systems and the local amenities, but as time passed our enthusiasm grew less. We soon learned to distinguish between the few serious enquirers and the much higher proportion of those who merely were curious to see the inside of other people's houses.

In the latter category we became convinced that there were many people who regarded house viewing as a pleasant way of spending a day in the country.

We could imagine them in their suburban homes over breakfast on a Friday morning.

"There's a good weather forecast for the weekend, Mable. Why don't you nip down to the houseagents and collect a few orders to view."

"What a lovely thought, dear. Anywhere you fancy in particular?"

"How about Buckinghamshire? We could do a couple in the morning, have a nice lunch by the river and take in another couple in the afternoon."

When they arrived, trailing their children behind them, she would peer into the broom cupboards, feel the quality of the curtains and try out the armchairs to see if they were comfortable, while he would spend his time pottering around the garden, turning over the compost heap with his toe to check that it was coming along alright, and peering at the motor mower to establish whether it was a later model than the one he had at home. Then they would decide that it was either too small or too far from the station, or didn't have a good enough view, before dashing on to their next victim, leaving us feeling inadequate and wondering how we could ever have come to take the house in the first place.

Twice we got to the point where it was simply a matter of serious purchasers raising a mortgage and twice it fell through because they could not, and back it went on the market again.

Finally I was alone in the house one morning trying to finish a rather difficult passage in a book I was writing when a young couple arrived at the door unannounced.

Could they see over the house? No, they had no order to view. They just happened to have been passing and saw the 'For Sale' notice.

"I don't think you'll like it," I found myself saying grumpily. "Very damp you know. Full of flies in the summer. Why don't you go and look at the other house for sale. It's just down the road on the left."

They remained undeterred.

As I showed them round grudgingly I laid it on good and thick. With ghoulish glee I demonstrated to them the awkwardness of the linen cupboard door, the window in the spare room which always jammed and the draught under the front door.

Two days later we had a letter from their solicitors saying that they were holding a cheque for the full asking price and how soon would it be possible to exchange contracts.

The morning after that we had a letter from Nigel King, the factor for Murthly Estates, saying that he was drawing up a lease for Rohallion in our name and asking when might we expect to move in.

3

WE ARRIVED up in Scotland again at the end of February, taking with us my two step-children, Fiona and Neil, and our own two, Charlie and Jo-Jo, and immediately drove them over to look at their new home.

Nigel King met us at the front door with the keys.

"All yours," he said, handing over a bunch of ironmongery which would not have looked out of place dangling from the belt of a medieval gaoler. "I think this one fits the front door," he added selecting one quite six inches long and weighing, I judged, around the half pound mark. Used to a little Yale key which Diana constantly had difficulty in finding in the bottom of her handbag, it came as quite a shock.

A moment later the children had rushed through the door and disappeared from view so that all we could hear were their distant cries as they called to each other excitedly to come and examine each new discovery. We strolled through the downstairs rooms with Nigel discussing small points connected with the handing over of the property until we finally came to the kitchen. Nigel was just discoursing, somewhat without conviction I thought, on the virtues of having a fifty year old Esse cooker and water heater combined, when peace was broken by an unearthly jangling of bells like some unholy carillon.

"Ah," he said. "It would seem that the children have discovered that the old bells still work." Indeed they had. Each of the main rooms were still fitted with Victorian bell pulls which when operated caused one or other of a dozen or so clappers in the passage outside the kitchen to oscillate wildly. "The novelty will soon wear off," he added philosophically. I may say it was a long time before it did.

A quarter of an hour later Nigel took his departure and we

were left alone to wrestle with the new problems inherent in adapting ourselves to spacious living.

The first and most pressing matter was the question of furnishing the place.

We had been told, and in our experience we had no reason to disbelieve it, that there was no difficulty in buying really large pieces of furniture at give away prices.

"Nobody wants vast sideboards and dining room tables to seat a dozen," a helpful friend had comforted us. "Go to any country house sale and you'll find they are giving the stuff away."

My mother of course took the opposite view and I must sadly admit that on this occasion she proved to be right. To give some idea of the problem, apart from the large reception rooms, our own bedroom measured twenty-four feet by eighteen so that when we tried to furnish it with pieces we had brought up from the south it looked as if they had come out of a doll's house.

Nor did I prove particularly adept when it came to the business of bidding at the many auctions which we attended.

One occasion in particular nearly proved disastrous. We were in need of certain small items for our garden, like a wheelbarrow and a scythe. Normally I would have gone to an ironmonger's shop and simply bought what I wanted but I had developed the sale mentality and was determined to find a bargain if I possibly could. It was therefore with great interest that I heard that my old friend, Andy Clark, was giving up his farm and having a sale of the farm effects.

There is an air of festivity about a farm sale, particularly when the vendor is a popular figure in the district. Neighbours dress up in their Sunday best; to help matters along one of the outhouses is fitted up as a temporary bar and everybody considers it as part of their neighbourly obligations to come along and lend support.

Moreover it is a matter of some honour that a purchaser should not appear to be too mean in the bidding. When the seller receives the final reckoning of who has bought what he likes to see that his friends have rallied round and given him a fair price.

This sense of comradeship does not however alter the rules

of the auction as they apply between the potential buyer and the auctioneer. If, for example, there is a tractor up for sale the first overtures of the auctioneer are ignored as beneath notice.

"What am I bid for this very fine tractor. You have seen it for yourselves, gentlemen. It is in first class condition. Only bought last year and in prime working order. What am I bid? Shall we start at a thousand pounds?"

Complete silence.

"Very well then eight hundred as the starting price."

Complete silence.

The auctioneer might have to come down to a hundred pounds before he gets a bid whilst he berates the buyers for their stinginess.

When the bidding starts, however, it is a brisk affair. Bids jump by a hundred at a time as people start lifting their fingers or touching their hats in a language which only they and the auctioneer understand. The bid which is eventually successful will often be far above the first asking price but the ritual has been observed.

It took me a long time to get used to this procedure and I used to attract curious looks when I jumped in with a bid too soon, fearful lest the auctioneer would lose patience and withdraw the item I wanted.

I was chatting to Andy Clark before his sale started and wishing him luck. There was a good attendance, the sun shone and there was the sound of laughter from the beer tent. But Andy looked worried. He fiddled with his pipe and nervously hitched up his trousers over his not inconsiderable stomach.

"There's one thing bothering me," he said. "It's my Land Rover. I've been thinking maybe I'd have got a better price if I'd sold it privately. Most of them here have already got a Land Rover and they'll no be needin' twa. Besides that I'm not sure I want to sell it at a'. She's a danged good yin."

"Well I must say I've just come for a wheelbarrow," I said. "Not that I wouldn't mind having your Land Rover if I could afford it. Now if it had been an eight foot wardrobe or a big sofa . . ."

"I'll tell you what," said Andy. "Give a hand with the bidding as a favour to me. No need to go too high but if there's someone really needing it you could maybe push him up a bit."

"I'll see what I can do," I promised. Just then the auctioneer climbed onto a hay cart and opened the proceedings.

So far as I can remember I got my wheelbarrow and a few other things I bid for besides and was well satisfied with my purchases. Then, the small items being disposed of, the auctioneer climbed down from his perch and led the way to a nearby field where all the farm machinery was set out.

The first to come under the hammer was the Land Rover. The usual battle of wits started again with the auctioneer calling for a bid of five hundred pounds, rapidly dropping the price in the face of stony silence with which his blandishments were greeted. At two hundred, mindful of my promise to Andy, I jumped in. At once there was a flurry of interest. "Two hundred I'm bid. Two fifty, three hundred. That's more like it, gentlemen. Three hundred and fifty. Any advance on three fifty." Confidently I extended four fingers in the air. "Four hundred. I'm bid four hundred. Any advance on four hundred." There was dead silence.

A moment later the auctioneer banged his gavel down on the table.

"Sold to the big gentleman at the back for four hundred pounds. A very good bargain if I may say so, sir." The little ripple of applause did nothing to shake me out of my stunned disbelief.

That was not the end of my disastrous day.

After the sale I drove my new acquisition away, trying to fool myself that what I wanted most in the world was a good-going Land Rover. Diana, equally in a state of shock, followed behind in our own car. On the way home, unused to the controls I stepped rather sharply on the brakes at a T-junction and Diana ran slap into my back, making a large dent in her radiator.

In spite of it all, however, it was one of the best purchases I ever made. She was to prove as Andy had said 'a danged good yin.'

It was at another farm sale that I first met "The Brooner". His real name I eventually discovered was Ian Brown but I have never heard him called anything else but "The Brooner".

A sale of any sort gives the Brooner as much delight as a debutante would get from attending her first ball. But nobody could look less like a debutante than the Brooner. He is a thick set man running slightly to flesh from the days when he was a champion in the heavy events at the highland games. His rugged face bears a constant expression of sardonic amusement and he dresses with just the right degree of respectable gentility as to disguise the fact that he is one of the shrewdest dealers in the county.

As I said I first met him at a farm sale.

"Would there be anything in particular that you're after," he asked, sizing me up speculatively as if making up his mind if there was anything I was wearing which he might make a bid for.

"Well I was thinking of trying for some buckets and there are one or two lots of junk I might be interested in." Everyone who has attended these sort of sales will be familiar with the practice of auctioneers of offering job lots so that if, for example, you want say a plastic bowl you also have to take with it a cracked tooth mug, a box full of marbles and a couple of unmatched flower vases.

I was soon to learn that nothing was too small to merit the Brooner's attention. He examined the few bits and pieces I had thought about bidding for with all the gravity of an art dealer assessing the genuineness of a Gainsborough.

"Leave it to me and don't you go bidding now or you'll have to pay ower muckle," he said severely. I didn't see him until the next day when he turned up at the house with the required articles.

"How much?" I asked. The amount seemed laughably small.

"Oh I've taken my profit alright," he said as he piled everything out on the doorstep. "Give your missus my regards," he shouted as he drove off. "There's forty ewes going cheap up the glen and I'll have to hurry if I'm not to miss them." That was by no means the last deal I was to do with the Brooner.

Our main preoccupation however was to get sufficient furniture to make the house habitable. Beds were easy enough in spite of a hang-up Diana had about not buying secondhand mattresses, but carpets and curtains were much more difficult. Even quite small carpets seemed to us exorbitantly expensive and large ones quite out of the question.

One day in Love's very fine furniture emporium in Perth I noticed in the antique department that they had a nice enough carpet on the floor of the showroom.

16

"I don't suppose you want to get rid of that," I asked casually.

"Certainly, sir," replied the salesman, "I think we could let you have that at a special price. Shall we say £2,000?"

"I'll have to think about it," I said desperately trying to save face.

The solution to the problem came unexpectedly. Diana and I were pottering around in the little local antique shop in Dunkeld when Mr. Stanley, the owner, came in. Like many other successful businessmen in Scotland he was a Pole who had come over with the Polish forces during the war and never gone back to his native land. Now he had a string of antique shops in various parts of the country and a large warehouse in Glasgow.

"I don't suppose in the course of your travels you come across any really large carpets?" I said without much hope.

"Carpets," he said, drawing himself up to his full height of five foot and a bit. "Carpets are my speciality."

"For very little money," I added hastily.

"Of course," he said, "for very little money."

And he was as good as his word. He came up to the house to assess our requirements and immediately took charge.

"Why not furnish the dining room?" he asked belligerently.

"You find me a ten foot sideboard, a big leaf table and maybe a matching set of a dozen chairs at a price I can afford and it will be done."

"I find them," he said, nodding vigorously.

Three days later he arrived perched behind the wheel of a huge lorry and, jumping out of the cab, let down the tailboard with a Continental flourish.

Mr. Stanley dispensed with such luxuries as men to help with loading and unloading.

"Take an end!" he shouted, and a moment later I was struggling under the weight of an enormous mahogany sideboard while he hoisted his end with practised ease.

To get this monster piece of furniture into the house and round the sharp turn into the dining room appeared at first sight to be an impossibility but my new friend masterminded the operation with all the skill of a Captain bringing the *Queen Elizabeth* in to dock.

When it was finally installed he patted it proudly.

"£25 O.K."

It was certainly O.K.

A fine set of high backed chairs followed, a great rectangular polished table and finally, his *pièce de résistance*, a twenty-five foot flowered carpet which he assured me had been designed by Queen Mary.

It never seemed to occur to him that I would question his good taste and he was quite right. Everything was just what we had been looking for.

When he told me the prices I could hardly believe my luck.

I asked him how he did it and he tapped his nose mysteriously.

"I have what you call good smell," he said.

With the help of Mr. Stanley and some welcome additions provided by my mother, the once empty rooms started to take on a personality of their own and we were able to turn our attention to other problems.

High on the list was the need for some help in the house and here again we appeared at first to be up against it.

Our nearest village is Dunkeld which is three miles away at the bottom of a steep hill. It seemed to be the most promising place to begin looking and we started asking everyone we met if they had any ideas, but the answer was usually the same.

Dunkeld is in fact two little townships. On the south side of the bridge which crosses the River Tay is Birnam which maintains a sturdy independence from Dunkeld proper on the other side of the water. Both are well known as tourist centres and have more than their fair share of hotels and boarding houses.

Indeed the line of houses along the road as you enter Birnam is popularly known as Hangman's Row, not from any criticism of the comfort they offer to the weary traveller, but from the proliferation of gibbet-like posts from which almost every house hangs its sign indicating that they take in guests. In consequence of all this activity the demand for domestic help, particularly in the tourist season, is virtually inexhaustible.

One day Diana was chatting to an acquaintance in the grocer's and put the usual question. Did she know anyone?

"Well," she said, "there's Mary Flanders. Such a splendid woman. She is on her own with three children to raise and a tower of strength in the church; but I don't know how she gets through what she has to do every day as it is."

I must say that I did not think it very promising when Diana reported the conversation to me.

"I don't think we could live up to all that splendidness," I said. "Jo-Jo came out with a new word the other day. I am pretty sure it was 'bloody' but it may have been even worse."

Just the same we thought it was worth a shot and the next morning we both went down to her house, lending each other mutual support in our negotiations with this formidable lady.

When Mary came to the door, however, she did not at all fit in with the picture we had conjured up of her as the cross between the old woman who lived in a shoe and Ena Sharples. She was much younger than we had expected, with a merry smile and an air of engaging frankness.

Yes, she said she was looking for morning work, and yes, if we could just give her time to take off her apron she could come up right away and see if she thought she could manage the job.

I have often said since that we didn't hire Mary – she hired us. She took one look at the house, put her hands firmly on her hips and said, "Ma Gawd. You certainly need somebody to sort this lot out. I'll start first thing the morn."

So we entered into a happy relationship which has now lasted for over ten years. She was soon to become our friend and most trusted counsellor. She was also a champion hair-touch setter of mousetraps, an art to which she applied herself with true devotion – as Charlie's sketch shows.

4

As OUR more pressing problems began to solve themselves we had more time to look around us and discover something about our new surroundings.

Although I had spent some of my youth at my mother's home near Blairgowrie, only fifteen miles away, and paid frequent visits there since, I had never really got to know Dunkeld. From my part of the country it was not on the road to anywhere unless perhaps Inverness, but even then you did not have to go through the village.

We had moved into Rohallion in two stages. I had formed the entire advance party and for the first few days had slept there in a sleeping bag until such time as it became feasible to bring up the rearguard which consisted of all the rest of the family. It was a few days I used to good advantage.

I am a person who likes pubs. It is a liking I have acquired through many years in Fleet Street where a pub is not only a place for relaxation but a place where much of a journalist's day to day business is transacted, having an atmosphere much more conducive to constructive thought than the soullessness of a noisy newspaper office.

The attitude towards pubs in Scotland is, however, somewhat different. There is not the classlessness of the English pub, particularly in the country districts. Tweedy men with loud voices and yellow labradors do not meet there of a Sunday morning to exchange the news of the week and chat with the locals as they did in Buckinghamshire. My mother for example, who is a pretty fast lady when it comes to drawing the cork out of a gin bottle in her own home, regards going to a pub as a rather daring adventure. To many of her contemporaries it would be unthinkable.

Indeed until quite recent times it was rare indeed to see women in pubs at all. They were not so much places for relaxation but places where men went to get down to the serious business of drinking. Many of them – too many – made little effort to provide the sort of comfort which makes for a happy family evening out. A dart board, a few wooden tables and a large bar were the essentials. Times are changing and there are now many charming and hospitable inns to attract even the most fastidious traveller, but the habits of the locals do not change so easily. For many of them the pub is still strictly male territory.

On my first few nights on my own at Rohallion, rather than sit at home gazing into an empty fireplace, I undertook some serious research into the problem of finding a pub which would meet with my not too exacting standards. It was an enjoyable way of passing the time but at first the results were not encouraging. Admittedly it was still out of season but there is something off-putting about a bar where one feels guilty of distracting the barmaid from her knitting or her absorption in some exciting paperback, to order a drink. My ideal is an unpretentious place where the proprietor himself runs the bar and attracts a circle of congenial customers. There is no quicker or pleasanter way of getting under the skin of somewhere than to be accepted in such a pub. It is like belonging to a good club.

I have gone to some length to give my views on pubs because when I finally discovered the Taybank Hotel it was to play an important part in our lives.

The Taybank is a modest enough establishment, painted white with about a dozen bedrooms and, as its name suggests enjoys a lovely setting overlooking the Tay – a river so noble that it is said that when the Romans first observed it from the heights above Dunkeld their commander exclaimed, "Behold, the Tiber!"

To describe Derek Reid, the proprietor, is not such an easy matter.

Although he must now be in his thirties with a pretty wife and four young children, he preserves an air of boyish innocence which belies his years and responsibilities. He also has a sense of humour which over the years has been a source of amusement and exasperation to his long suffering customers. The unwary tourist asking when the bar closes is likely to receive the unhelpful reply of "About November" and, if Diana were to ask for more ice she would be likely to receive enough rocks in her glass to sink the *Lusitania*. When Diana's father, a gentleman of the old school, came to stay with us shortly after we moved into Rohallion, he had the temerity to ask for a slice of lemon in his gin and tonic. Derek remedied the omission without comment. When we came to leave, however, he ostentatiously picked the lemon out of the glass and, popping it into a small plastic bag, remarked without any change of expression, "I'll just keep this in case you may be needing it tomorrow."

In spite of his determination to keep the customers in their place, however, he is helpfulness itself if one has any problems, and we had plenty, even if they were only simple matters like getting someone to fix a broken window. Tradesmen are, I suppose, the same the world over. If we wanted some small job done we would resort to the yellow pages of the telephone book and ring up the nearest address.

"We're very busy" a voice would answer at the other end. "Can it wait until Thursday?" Then Thursday would come and go with no sign of anybody. An appeal to Derek would, however, produce instant results. A quiet word with somebody in the bar or a quick telephone call, and the next day the job would be done. In a very short space of time the Taybank was christened "The Branch Office" . . .

So it was that with the rallying round of a lot of new friends we gradually began, in Mary's words, to "get oorsells sorted" and discover bit by bit the history of our new property.

The origins of Rohallion as I came to discover them proved to be as fascinating as the strange design of the house itself.

During the first half of the last century the great landowning family of Stewart had an agent – factor as he is called in Scotland, who was a man of remarkable talents. His name, Conde, is perpetuated in the name of the firm of Perth solicitors which he founded, but in his day he was known as an amateur architect of considerable talent. He built several country houses on classical lines but he was only really happy when he could indulge his own flights of fancy. Fortunately the laird of the vast Murthly Estates, Captain Sir William Drummond Stewart, was the sort of man to whom Conde's taste for the grandiose appealed and it was he who commissioned him to build Rohallion.

William Stewart himself was a very remarkable man. Born a second son he must have considered his chance of ever succeeding to the rich Murthly Estates to be remote. His elder brother had only to marry and produce an heir for that chance to disappear forever. When he was seventeen his father bought him a commission in the fashionable Sixth Dragoon Guards and in doing so considered that he had discharged his parental obligations.

William was very much a man's man. He fought in Spain and Portugal and was one of Wellington's lieutenants at the Battle of Waterloo. Without the excitements of the war with Napoleon, however, he found the army a dull business and retired on half pay to pursue his passion for sport in the hunting grounds of Europe.

On one of his rare visits to Scotland he was out walking with his friend Lord George Glenlyon near Blair Atholl when they came across an extraordinarily beautiful girl, her skirts pulled up above her knees as she trampled blankets in a wash tub. Not very much of a ladies' man, the sight so overcame the bold Captain that he took immediate steps to get to know her, with the result that she bore him a son nine months later.

Horrified at this unexpected outcome he did the decent thing by marrying her. Then he installed her in a modest flat in Edinburgh with their son, while he himself took a fast boat to America. There is no evidence that he ever saw her again although his son was ultimately to inherit the estate.

William Stewart and the Wild West took to each other immediately. He loved the rigorous life and the magnificent sport the country offered and he rapidly became one of the best known amongst the more adventurous of the European aristocracy who used the country as their playground.

When he first came across herds of buffalo he was ecstatic. Thinking of Rohallion where he one day planned to make his home, he turned in the saddle to his hunting companion the great William Sublette, and declared that he would not be satisfied until they had captured some of the animals alive and shipped them back to Scotland.

"Don't you know Captain," Sublette replied, "it is quite

impossible to keep buffalo without Indians to look after them."

"In that case," declared Stewart, "I'll ship some Indians back home as well."

So in due course, the Captain being the sort of man who always got his way, a herd of buffalo arrived at Rohallion, accompanied by a couple of dozen seasick and bewildered Red Indians.

Unexpectedly William's elder brother had died without issue and he suddenly found himself heir to all the estates and the baronetcy. More importantly, for the first time in his life he had plenty of money, and he now spent freely in building Rohallion house as well as a great stone walled compound for his buffalo. For the Indians he had less consideration. He allocated them to a portion of wild hillside where they could pitch their tepees and left them to look after themselves and the buffalo as best they could.

Of course such goings on were the subject of the utmost excitement amongst the estate workers and the Dunkeld villagers. To begin with all went well. Sir William, during the first summer after the arrival of the animals, gave the locals real value. He would have his Indians herd the buffalo down to the low ground alongside the Tay where he would gallop after them dressed in his Wild West hunting garb and whirling his lassoo above his head. One wonders whether the locals were more impressed by the thundering of the beasts or by the silent dark-skinned Indians who looked on impassively.

Alas, the whole great scheme was to end in failure. With the coming of winter and the long nights of wet cold, the Indians in their tents caught pneumonia and died off one by one. The unsupervised buffalo broke out of their pens and ravaged the countryside to the terror of the inhabitants. Long after Sir William himself was dead there were still buffalo roaming the Perthshire hills.

Soon after we arrived at Rohallion we climbed up to what has ever since been known as Buffalo Park and looked in wonder at the remains of Sir William's enclosures. It was not difficult to imagine that the ghosts of those vast animals, so unexpectedly removed from their native environment, still roamed restlessly on the pine-clad slopes.

Although there is no record that Sir William ever lived much at Rohallion after he had inherited the great family seat of Murthly Castle, he left his mark on it in other ways. It was he who had the little loch artificially created and planted it round with rhododendrons, and he who planted the great trees which we had remarked on when we first stopped in front of the house.

Did he perhaps meet the great Scottish plant collector David Douglas in Canada and did Douglas give him the seeds of the fir which is called after him to bring back to Scotland and plant at Rohallion. It is a romantic thought.

The Douglas fir is one of the grandest of all our fir trees and shares with the silver fir the distinction of being a true conifer. It is, of course, not a native to this country although it is closely related to the pine. Nor in fact was it 'discovered' by David Douglas. That distinction goes to another Scotsman, Archibald Menzies who first identified it on Vancouver Island in 1791 over thirty-five years before Douglas sent the first seeds back to this country. The tree's Latin name *Pseudotsuga menziesii* gives credit where it is due.

Around our great Douglas fir the cones lie thick on the ground and we gather them to burn on the fire when they give off a delightful smell. The needles too, if you rub them between your fingers emit a lemon-like scent.

Sir William's mark is left in another peculiarity of the house. When he created the loch on the west side of the house he ordered that there should be no windows overlooking it as he did not like the servants to watch him while he was fishing. Mindful of the needs of later generations, however, he had spaces for the windows built into the walls and then blocked up so that to open them up again would not be a difficult matter. This was largely done by our predecessors in the house but there still remain a few to be opened up and each year I resolve to have it done. One day I will.

Queen Victoria records in her *Journal of our life in the Highlands*, a visit to Rohallion – "Sir William Stewart's delightful hunting lodge" – so it would seem that he regarded it as a place where he could occasionally get away from the pressures of living in his grand castle and perhaps relive again some of the joys of the simple life which had appealed to him so much in his pioneering days. So that life would not be too onerous, however, he had the hills and woods surrounding the

27

house dotted with delightful little loggias. These beautifully built summer houses with their intricately patterned wood ceilings are still in perfect condition and were to be a great source of joy to us for picnics on our rambles round our 'estate'.

The generations which have followed the adventurous Sir William have left little mark on the place. At some stage the drawing room has been enlarged and a porch built onto the front of the house. It was perhaps the same hand which installed a bow window from which you can step out on to the west terrace. A keen sportsman from the past has erected an elaborate stone shelter on the east side of the house, to house a rod rack and adorned with an immense stag's head wrought in iron while yet another tenant has caused a fine headstone to be erected under the old rhododendron to mark the resting place of 'Toby' who departed this life 1st Feb 1894.

Even the names of the people who once enjoyed this lovely house are now largely forgotten, but one has survived the passing of time. High up on the hillside and clearly seen from the terrace there is a structure which looks, improbable though it may appear, to be a bridge with a succession of arches. Struggle through the shoulder high bracken up the steep hillside, and as you draw near the improbable becomes reality. It *is* a bridge. A massive drystone affair with three arches and a castellated parapet. It spans a small gorge far too insignificant to warrant such prodigious architectural effort.

Indeed on the first occasion when Charlie and I hauled ourselves, panting on to the bridge itself it was to see that it had little use except perhaps as an easy passage for sheep and deer on their way across the rough hillside. As we regained our breath – for the climb at any rate for someone of my girth, is quite an arduous one – we speculated whose hands could have heaved all those great stones into place and for what possible purpose. Charlie, with his tendency to telescope history, gave it as his opinion that it had been built by the Romans. I, with little conviction, thought it might have been once part of a drovers' road.

At the first opportunity I sought out Jimmy Wemyss to ask him about it.

"Oh that is Allen's Bridge," he said as if it explained everything.

"And who," I persisted, "was Allen?"

"Allen was the butler at Rohallion for many years," Jimmy explained. "He worked for old Lady Carnegie. Her that bought the boat for the loch. Well this Allen was a strange man. He never went out on his time off but every afternoon when her Ladyship was resting, he used to climb up there and add a few more stones to his bridge. It took him all of twenty years before it was finished. He died a happy man. It's not everybody achieves what they set out to do," added Jimmy reflectively.

I thought Jimmy was probably one of them but I did not say so. Instead I marvelled at the industry of one man and wondered if it would have given him satisfaction to know that his name would live on after he himself had been long forgotten.

It was fun this gradual finding out about the house we lived in, like developing a slowly maturing friendship. There were some in the village who could bring the past into sharp focus. One of them was Stewart Robertson.

Stewart was, and still is I am happy to report, a very remarkable character. He is a master builder and until he retired a couple of years ago he set off each Monday morning in his van at four o'clock in the morning to report in time for his work with a big constructional firm in Oban – a matter of eighty miles away. He would work there all week, living in a caravan, and then return on Friday evening to his home in Dunkeld. I would have thought this was rather an uncomfortable way of life but it suited him. The firm for whom he worked had given him a good job when times were hard and he felt he owed them a loyalty. At the same time he could not bear not to spend his spare time amongst his friends in his own village. This way he made the best of both worlds.

Most interesting to me was the fact that he had been born and brought up on Rohallion and I spent many a happy evening with him sitting in the Taybank exchanging drinks while he talked of the old days.

As a boy he had walked to school in Bankfoot which is fully three miles away. He did this barefoot on unmetalled roads, but the soles of his feet became so hardened that he did not feel the sharp stones.

"Of course I used to cheat when I could," he confessed to me one evening. "There was a farmer who kept a pony in a field ust by our cottage and I often used to 'borrow' it for the day without his knowing, and ride it bareback to school over the fields."

He remembered when the Rohallion stables, which lie about half a mile from the house, were not desolate and empty but full of horses to pull the carriages for the folk at the big house and there were magnificent gardens laid out between the stables and the house, which produced all manner of vegetables and flowers. Today clumps of bright delphiniums struggling through the undergrowth and some rotted trelliswork is all there is to show, and the gardener's house was pulled down soon after we took possession because it had fallen into a dangerous state of disrepair.

One Saturday afternoon I took Stewart up to look at the place he had known so well as a child. As we peered in through the leaning stable doors, flocks of pigeons flew out over our heads.

Much to Stewart's joy, on the woodwork surrounding the stalls, long gone grooms had written their names in large rounded letters.

"Jimmy Morrison, 3rd horseman 1912," he read. "I remember him fine. Killed in the war. The Great War that was."

He shook his head sadly. "Fine days they were," he murmured and so I suppose they were in retrospect, though there are few people today who would put up with the long hours, one day's holiday a year – New Year's Day – and all for a few shillings a week.

Another regular at the Branch Office who proved to be an inexhaustible source of information about the district in which we had come to live was Peter Watson.

Peter is small and wiry enough to be a steeplechase jockey with ankles and wrists so small that you can easily encircle them with finger and thumb. His voice makes up for his small stature. He speaks with a sort of rattle not unlike a Scottish Schnozzle Durante and when he gives forth he includes everybody in the bar as his audience.

"I'm the Provost of Dunkeld," he said to me when I first met him.

"Is he really?" I asked Derek when Peter had gone off for his midday meal.

"Perhaps if we had a Provost in Dunkeld Peter would get the job. As it is we don't – fortunately."

Peter and Derek are great friends but Derek can never resist teasing him, to which Peter reacts by abusing him at the top of his voice.

Peter knows as much about Dunkeld and the district as anyone. He has been a slater, as his father was before him, ever since he was a lad and never away from the district except when he joined up during the war. Now he is the boss of his own business with the headaches of V.A.T., P.A.Y.E., and the other inescapable responsibilities of modern life, but he still spends a fair proportion of his time scrambling about on other people's roofs.

Peter claims to have worked on every big house for miles around and to have known the people who lived in them over the last fifty years or so, but there is none for whom he has a greater admiration than the Dukes of Atholl.

The Atholl lands extend from Dunkeld to far north of Pitlochry and Peter likes to tell the story of the present Duke's great-uncle calling in to visit Peter's father in his little cottage in Cathedral Street. It was before the days when indoor sanitation was considered normal but just the same the Duke was shocked to discover that the Watson family had recourse to the bottom of the garden.

"I'll have that put right straight away Watson," he declared.

Peter's father was greatly alarmed. His take-home pay was in the order of four shillings a week and he feared that if a lavatory was put in his house the rent would be raised.

"I can't afford to pay any more Your Grace," he said. "We'll just carry on the way we have always done."

The Duke fixed him with a stern stare from under his bushy eyebrows. "Watson," he declared "You'll never pay a single penny more rent while I am alive." And he was as good as his word.

Peter still lives in the same cottage, now taken over by the National Trust for Scotland. It is one of a row of little houses which line the lane leading up to the gates of the cathedral and they have all been restored to the state of when they were first built in 1740. Inside however they are as modern as can be. The old Duke would have been pleased.

If Scottish villages do not have the same immediate appeal to the visitor as their counterparts in the South of England there are many with their own particular charm, and Dunkeld is one of them. It is set almost exactly in the middle of Scotland. Inverness is a hundred miles to the north over the Grampians while to the south is the rolling rich countryside of Central Scotland. It is perhaps because of its strategic position on the Highland Line that Dunkeld has played such an important part in history. It was to Dunkeld that the first Culdee monks came over from Iona to set up a Christian community. Towards the end of the 6th century they built a wattle monastery on the banks of the Tay. Three hundred years later that great Scottish King, Kenneth MacAlpin had it rebuilt in stone. Later still, in 1127, King David created a Bishopric there and raised the Monastery to the status of a cathedral, a status it has enjoyed ever since.

How, one wonders, did William Shakespeare gain his local knowledge of Dunkeld's twin village Birnam on the other side of the river. There are few schoolboys who cannot quote Macbeth when he declares: 'Fear not, till Birnam wood do come to Dunsinane'. Glamis Castle lies fifteen miles to the east and Dunsinane Hill which is about half that distance even today scarcely merits an entry on the most detailed of maps. Most of the great oaks that Shakespeare knew of, which stood on the river bank at Birnam, have long since fallen to storm or the woodcutter's axe, but at least one remains, a gnarled and majestic link with the past.

During Shakespeare's time zealous religious reformers desecrated the Cathedral. Later, in 1689, it was almost completely destroyed during the Battle of Dunkeld when the supporters of James VII finally won a victory over Cromwell's Covenanters at great cost to life and property.

Surprisingly for such an important place there was no bridge across the Tay at Dunkeld until one which has been in use ever since was finally built in 1809 by the great Thomas Telford who was responsible for such masterpieces of engineering as the Menai suspension bridge which links Anglesey to the mainland.

Dunkeld, in spite of its importance in political and religious history, has never developed industrially. Perth, fifteen miles further down the river, where the Kings of Scotland came once to be crowned in Scone Palace, has grown to the size of a considerable city, whilst Dunkeld has continued to sleep on quietly. The vast lorries which hurtle through it on their way up and down the A.9 and the procession of cars, dragging behind them trailers and caravans which drive nose to tail during the summer months, will soon be no more. Plans which have been discussed for over a quarter of a century to bypass the village have at last become a reality and nobody will be more glad than the inhabitants when the new road is completed for Dunkeld is a friendly place which does not like to be merely a milestone on the route of the heedless tourist. They prefer the visitor to tarry a while, to poke around the quiet corners and enjoy the feeling of history.

At Rohallion, although our driveway opened off the main road, we were sufficiently remote not to be troubled by the streams of traffic which became more and more of a flood as spring turned to summer. Sometimes on damp nights as we lay in bed we would hear the distant growl of the heavy laden lorries as they changed gear to climb the steep hill out of Birnam but this added to rather than detracted from our feeling of being comfortably cut off from the outside world.

5

OF COURSE what we should have done that first year at Rohallion was to have concentrated on the business of fitting ourselves into our new surroundings to the exclusion of all else.

Unfortunately in our first flush of pride of possession we were liberal with our invitations to even the most casual of acquaintances.

"Do drop in when you are passing," Diana and I would urge and out would come the address books and our whereabouts carefully noted but we were still always faintly surprised later to receive a telephone call to say that they were in Perth or Edinburgh or Inverness and had worked it out on the map that they could be with us in comfortable time for lunch. Anybody touring Scotland would almost inevitably pass our gates at some stage or another.

Many of what we came to call 'the passing trade' would avail themselves a bed for a night or two so that one party would hardly have departed before the next lot arrived. Diana and Mary toiled with mountains of sheets and pillowcases and the endless preparation of meals whilst I ran up mammoth bills at my wine and spirit merchants. My literary output dwindled until finally in the height of the summer it dried up altogether as more and more people made demands on us as not altogether reluctant hosts.

To be quite truthful we both quite enjoyed the novelty of having a floating population in the house after our cramped quarters in Buckinghamshire and took a delight in showing them around the countryside which we were just beginning to know ourselves. It was, however, not very sound economically.

House guests divide themselves roughly into one of two categories. The first are frankly pains in the neck. From the moment they decant themselves from their car outside the front door until the moment they leave they make the same demands upon one as if it were a first class hotel. They expect their meals to be served exactly on time and their individual tastes catered for. Like Jack Spratt who could eat no fat and his wife who could eat no lean they practically write their own demanding menus every day and certainly expect their amusements to be planned down to the last exhausting detail. If they decide to visit a stately home in the district they want to know, not only precisely how to get there, but how much it will cost them and what they will need in their picnic basket which will save them from having to rely on the usually very adequate restaurant facilities. They make one feel riddled with guilt if the children wake them too early in the morning or if the day they planned to go walking turns out to be rainy. Fortunately this type is comparatively rare but still, until we grew wiser, frequent enough to have made us very wary over the years of having people to stay whom we don't know well.

The second general category are quite the opposite. They arrive bearing embarrassingly rich gifts like bottles of whisky and *foie gras* from Fortnum and Mason. They disappear soon after breakfast, happily carrying off with them a selection of our children and return in the evening full of an enthusiasm which makes us feel that if the sun has shone it is entirely due to our excellent management. The evenings are filled with merriment and good conversation so that the following morning hangovers are brushed aside and we only feel glad that they are still with us to enjoy another day.

Perhaps our favourite visitors that first summer were John and Pat Bennett. John is a fine actor who at the time was starring in a television series as Billy Bush in "Market in Honey Lane" and his wife, Patricia Hastings, is still a name remembered in theatrical circles from the great days when she played as a juvenile in Noël Coward comedies. That she now only appears occasionally on the television screen is to my mind a loss.

To be quite truthful John and Pat are not the most restful people to be with. They positively crackle with energy and they only tolerate my habit of dozing off in an armchair after lunch as an amiable eccentricity. On their arrival for that first visit

John had hardly switched off the engine of his car before he had unloaded and pumped up a rubber dinghy and was half way across the loch with their son Jamie and our Charlie, who is his great friend, precariously perched in the stern, whilst Pat whirled round the house on a tour of inspection.

"Divine, darling, quite divine," I heard her saying to Diana as they swept past the door of my study where I was pouring myself a steadying drink. "Now we can get the paint for that top bedroom tomorrow and don't bother to ring anybody about that broken window. John can fix that. Then we can get down to . . ." Her voice died away as they shot off in another direction, leaving me with a feeling of relief that all those things I had been putting off for so long looked like getting done at last.

The great thing about the Bennetts is that they do not make one feel guilty about one's own inertia. Their enthusiasm for everything from climbing hills to late night poker games is inexhaustible and they carry one along with them. There were however occasions when John's do-it-yourself mania got out of hand.

One of the few things I am better at than John is catching fish. If he resented this he did not show it but there were several occasions when I saw him sneaking off down to the loch to put in a little quiet practice. He even persuaded Charlie to teach him the technique of fishing with a worm which is something a fly fishing purist like myself would consider pretty close to cheating.

One morning he returned from one of these clandestine expeditions looking almost smugly triumphant. It turned out that he had not caught the largest fish in the loch but he had managed to capture an enormous eel! Now nothing would satisfy him but that he must cook it and eat it. I tried to dissuade him but he would have none of it.

"The eel is the staple diet of London East Enders," he declared. "What's good enough for them is good enough for me," bearing his prize off to the kitchen.

Diana who is a cook of considerable distinction was appointed as assistant chef and much time was spent poring over a wide selection of cookery books. It was finally decided that they would not only cook it but jelly it in the traditional manner.

It was at this stage that they hit their first snag. The eel which had in the meantime been put in the kitchen sink was still swimming around in the most lively manner. Diana managed to capture it wearing rubber gloves and held it on the kitchen table while John hit it a succession of solid blows on the head. This merely had the effect of making it wriggle even more violently. Diana lost her hold whereupon it fell off the table and slithered across the floor, taking refuge under the electric cooker. From this point of vantage it peered out at them balefully as if defying them to recapture it.

At this moment I came through to the kitchen to see how they were getting on and was glad to see that even John was looking a trifle nonplussed.

"Don't you know," I told them scornfully, "that the only way to kill an eel is to cut the nape of the neck. That's where the backbone is near to the surface and can easily be broken." Delighted for once at being able to show off my superior knowledge, I advanced upon the unfortunate amphibian, dragged it from its refuge and again putting it on the table, deftly demonstrated the technique.

For a moment it lay quite still while John and Diana looked on with something pretty near to admiration. Then suddenly it started to perform the most incredible contortions thrashing about like a demented Loch Ness monster.

"Those are just the death throes," I said airily and hurriedly left the room. It looked very far from dead to me.

I kept well clear of the kitchen after that but it was quite obvious that things were not going too well. It was approaching lunch time so Pat and I called through that we were going down to the Branch Office and left them to it. Later, much later, they joined us there. They had the look of desperate people who will not admit that they are beaten. I noticed John broke his rule of never having large drinks in the middle of the day.

"We got it skinned and cut up and it's cooking beautifully," he reported without I thought very much confidence.

"The only thing," Diana added doubtfully, "the pieces still seemed to be wriggling."

"Nerves," I said comfortingly. "I must say I don't blame it."

That day we got Derek to get us some sandwiches. Nobody seemed to have the heart for much more cooking.

Sometime that afternoon it was taken off the stove and left to congeal in its coat of aspic. At six o'clock I poured them all a stiff drink in the drawing room and we trooped through to view the result.

Although I have all my life resolutely refused to eat eel I have often seen it displayed on stalls at the seaside or down the Mile End Road and even offered in smart West End restaurants. Sometimes it looked almost good enough to eat. This was far from the case with John and Diana's joint production. Bones stuck out of the aspic at all angles and the flesh looked an unappetizing dull grey. Worst of all the head had somehow got into the pot and it now eyed us reproachfully through its coat of jelly.

"Who's going to have the first taste?" said Diana with a gallant attempt at brightness.

John had turned the same grey shade as the eel.

"I think I will take you all out to dinner tonight," he said.

At least the cats fed very well for the next few days.

*   *   *

Two other very welcome guests were our friends Victor and Sally Briggs and they were put up in the room which my mother had so definitely stated to be haunted.

When it comes to the question of whether you believe in ghosts or not I am a 'don't know'. Twice as a boy I thought I saw a ghost. Once in half-wakefulness I saw a figure which seemed to flit from the end of my bed to the window and another time with my brother Gordon in the loft above the cart sheds of my father's farm. Neither time, however, could I be sure that it was not just a trick of light and there was no history of murder most vile or other legend to encourage conviction.

My mother on the other hand is a veteran seer of ghosts and a feeler of 'presences'. For good measure she has seen the Loch Ness Monster and who can deny the possibility of that. That saintly man the late Abbot of Fort Augustus at the end of Loch Ness saw it the whole time.

Indeed some of mother's ghosts are almost believable. Staying in one of the oldest inhabited castles in Scotland she announced one morning at breakfast that she had had a long conversation with a ghost the previous night. With a history of almost nine hundred ghost-free years her host was not unnaturally sceptical but when she described the figure she had seen he took her along a corridor to see a portrait of his grandfather which tallied exactly with her description.

Another rather more modern manifestation which she claims to have experienced was that whilst driving on a long straight stretch of road her car was suddenly violently rocked on the road as if being passed by another car at high speed. But there was no other traffic in sight. It was only after a similar phenomenon had been reported in the same place by a Director of the Bank of Scotland – a man not given to wild flights of fancy – that she was taken a little more seriously.

One of the local ghost stories which is hard to disprove concerns an uninhabited castle on an island in the middle of Clunie Loch which lies almost half way between Rohallion and my mother's house. It is the home so the story goes of a cowled monk who perversely will only appear to maiden ladies at midnight. The few hardy ladies who have ventured to spend a night on the island confirm that this is true. The alternative of course is to put their chastity in doubt.

My mother's conviction that the best guest bedroom at Rohallion was ghost ridden seemed to me to be one of her more improbable extravaganzas until one day we received a visit from a very old lady who had been brought up locally. Her grandson had rung up to ask if he could bring her to Rohallion where she had worked as a young girl.

They came to tea and were just leaving when she asked in a most matter of fact way how the ghost was getting on.

"Ghost?" I said at once interested. "I did not know there was a ghost."

"In that room up there," she said indicating the guest room. "A young Indian girl you know."

The story as she told it was that one of the Indians brought over by Sir William Stewart had been taken on as an undermaid by a sadistic housekeeper who treated her very cruelly. She beat her so frequently and kept her so short of food that she died and her restless spirit manifests itself from time to time by the sound of blows followed by wild screams.

As I have already said the room in question is so light and airy with a long window looking over the loch and a balcony on the garden side that of all the rooms in the house it is by far the least sinister. Just the same I purposely refrained from mentioning the ghost to guests about to sleep there. Even the most matter of fact people react unpredictably to any suggestion of the supernatural. I had in fact almost forgotten the story when Victor and Sally came to stay.

At breakfast after their first night I asked them how they had slept and it appeared not at all well.

"I was wakened by an odd noise," said Victor. "At first it sounded like plaster falling. Then when I was fully awake it sounded more like blows being struck and groaning. Are you sure you are not haunted?"

So I told him the story which pleased his imaginative nature greatly. I think he was rather disappointed when he and Sally were undisturbed for the rest of the week. Two more guests joined us the next weekend and on the first morning after their arrival Victor came down to breakfast in a high state of excitement. He had heard the ghost again.

This time he had distinctly heard cries and blows and a voice raised in anger. I thought at first that he was putting on an act for the benefit of the new arrivals when glancing across the breakfast table I was surprised to see that Diana was choking with what looked very like suppressed laughter. A moment later she rose from her chair and fled precipitately from the room.

The explanation came later.

"Didn't you see Rachel's eye?" she asked. Rachel and Hugh, which for obvious reasons are not their real names, were the other couple and Diana had been on the opposite side of the table to them. Two very intelligent but temperamental people, their marriage had been going through a sticky patch and we had asked them up in the hope that the peace of the countryside would help matters between them.

"They obviously had a set-to in their bedroom. Victor and his ghosts indeed! That eye will be a real shiner by lunch time, mark my words," Diana prophesied.

Later there were rather shame-faced confessions which spoilt one good ghost story. I am glad to say however that in their case the magic of Rohallion worked and by the end of their stay they were spending most of their time sitting close together on the lover's seat at the shady end of the terrace, holding hands and gazing into each other's eyes.

We have never had any complaints about the ghost since.

I don't know if the Scots are more ghost conscious than other races but we do seem to have an unconscionable number of houses which are supposed to be haunted round about us. Glamis Castle, the Queen Mother's old home which is about twenty miles away is alleged to have a thriving population of ghosts and there is a house on the way to Loch Tay in the opposite direction which is so haunted that nobody will live in it.

All in all our first summer at Rohallion was a lot of fun.

6

I am not now surprised to remember that my involvement with hens was my mother's idea. She has always had a few hens herself. It may have been that she got fed up with my always going away with a hatful of eggs whenever I visited her, or it may have been simply that she did not think I had enough trouble already, but it was certainly she who was the inspiration behind the whole crazy scheme.

In fact the first thinking was sound enough. It was simply that with fresh eggs in the shops, which were often not fresh at all, being so expensive and with there being a number of buildings out the back of the house which could serve as chicken houses, it would seem to be common sense to keep a few hens. I could foresee a situation where not only would we have splendid eggs but we would hatch our own chicks and kill off the old birds so that we would have a self-perpetuating flock and cut drastically on the house-keeping. They would be fed, of course, which is one of the greatest myths about hen keeping, on household scraps.

Perhaps, as has happened with so many money-making schemes which I have toyed with, it would never have got off the ground had it not been that we had gone to lunch at a neighbouring farm and discovered that they had a couple of dozen half grown chicks surplus to requirements.

We carried them home in a series of large hat boxes to find, by a stroke of great good fortune, that my elder brother Gordon had called in.

I should explain here something about my brothers. Gordon is a sheep farmer near Kirkmichael and my younger brother runs the old family house as a country house hotel outside Blairgowrie. They are as unalike as it is possible for brothers to be, Gordon is lean and hungry looking while John bears an uncanny resemblance both in face and figure to Benny Hill. They have however one thing in common. They both fancy themselves as practical men who can turn their hand to any job under the sun. John's particular forte, according to himself, is doing electrical work. A claim he established, so far as I can remember when we were both staying as boys in an imposing castle in Aberdeenshire. John volunteered to mend a fuse with the result that he knocked out the complete electrical system and the whole houseparty had to spend the weekend going about by candlelight. Gordon's passion is building things and he is never happier than when he is pulling something down and putting it up again. Over the years, by trial and error, they have become reasonably proficient and I take advantage of their vanity quite ruthlessly. The surest way of getting a visit from either of them is to mention that I have made a botch of some particular job and they appear, as if I had rubbed a magic lamp, anxious to prove what a duffer I am.

When, that afternoon, we proudly showed Gordon our chicks, he immediately decreed that they could not be kept shut in an outhouse but must have a proper hen run. Fortunately I had some rolls of wire netting, bought for no good reason at one of the many farm sales I had attended and, in a miraculously short space of time he had enclosed an area large enough to accommodate five times the number of birds.

Of course, as I might have guessed, that was by no means the end of the operation.

"Chickens must have perches to roost on," Gordon declared, "otherwise they grow up with crooked breastbones." I had not thought of that but next day he was back with the required lengths of wood, hammering away like a man possessed whilst I was sent scurrying off to buy a proper receptacle for them to drink water out of because we had soon discovered that the idiotic birds simply tipped over anything not specifically designed for the purpose. Finally the tea chests in which our books and china had arrived from the south were filled with hay and impressed into duty as makeshift nest boxes.

Only then were we finally in business as chicken farmers.

If we had expected instant eggs after all this cosseting, we were in for a considerable disappointment. They had a lot of growing to do yet. As they started to feather up, however, it began to become obvious even to an inexperienced eye, that many of them would never lay an egg at all for it appeared that, if anything there were more cocks than hens. Hard put to it to keep pace with their gross eating habits I was all for killing some of the cocks off and having them for Sunday lunch, but Diana would not hear of it. Woman's Lib. is not really her strong suit but she conceived the romantic, if rather Victorian, idea that every hen should have her own husband and there was nothing I could do to dissuade her.

Worse it soon appeared that they were not content with their enormous run and found ways of squeezing under Gordon's wire netting and disappearing into the woods, condescending only to come back when it was feeding time. In the end I gave up trying to keep them in and they became very free range hens indeed.

This in turn led to a new complication which dramatically altered Diana's views about the cocks.

I had always thought of hens, generically, as the most docile of birds which lived their lives peacefully pecking around the back door, the housewife's friends and a picture of domesticity.

Our cock birds did not subscribe to this romantic view. They took no notice of me as they regarded me as their chief food provider, but Diana started to complain that whenever she took out the washing to hang it on the green behind the hen run, the cocks were showing distinct signs of animosity.

Day by day the accounts grew more lurid.

"You'll have to do something about those cocks," she declared, one day over coffee. "One of them flew up my skirt this morning when I was doing the washing. I can still feel where he pecked me."

Jo-Jo aged four also declared herself to be in mortal fear of the cocks. Her solution was down-to-earth.

"Put um in the oven and cookum," she ordered. She was beginning to sound more like a Sioux chief every day.

"What you town-bred people don't understand is that they are just trying to be friendly," I said with a confidence born from being brought up on a farm. "Just shoo at them and they will run away."

Matters came to a head one morning as I was sitting at my typewriter when I heard loud shrieks coming from the back

quarters. I rushed out to find Diana and Jo-Jo perched on top of a high wall while one of the cocks strutted angrily below, crowing defiance and ruffling his burnished neck feathers. I took one look and collapsed with laughter.

The day of the cockerels rule of terror was, however, coming to an end.

Crisis point was reached when one morning after breakfast I went out to feed them as usual. As I entered the hen run one of the cocks rushed out at me, ruffling its feathers and dancing threateningly in the air. Outraged at this show of unwarranted hostility I put the toe of my shoe under it and lifted it fully fifteen feet to the other side of the hen run. In an instant it was back again as menacing as ever, its beady eyes literally red with suffused rage. I dumped the hen food hurriedly and beat an undignified retreat.

Back in the house I declared that indeed something must be done.

"Typical of a man," Diana sneered, "just because one of them went for you something has to be done! What do you think we have been putting up with all these weeks?"

It was at this stage that I realised that I was ill-equipped to deal with the emergency. I am not really squeamish. Out shooting I can readily put a wounded hare out of its agony and as a boy I used to hunt rats at night armed with nothing but a lantern and an old tennis racquet, but to do in one of my own cockerels was a different sort of problem. I have never mastered the art of wringing a bird's neck and the only times I have tried it has been at the risk of its head coming off in my hand. I considered the merits of shooting them but discarded the idea as being unsporting.

In the end I rang up my mother to ask her advice. After all she was supposed to be the expert.

I had to endure a certain amount of derision but in the end she took pity on us.

"Make sure they are shut in the henhouse tonight and I'll come over and do the job myself."

My mother is a woman of many talents but it had never occurred to me that wringing necks might be one of them.

When I focused the beam of my torch on the birds roosting on their perches they clucked uneasily but made no effort to move. In an instant my mother had grabbed the largest cock by the legs and putting two fingers round its neck gave a quick twist. A moment later it was dead and lying on the ground, its wings flapping in muscular spasms. Others followed in quick succession until only two remained.

"No wonder they were bad tempered," she declared. "With so many of them they had nothing to use up their energy on." So much for Diana's views on monogamy.

At the same time mother gave us some more advice on the gentle art of egg production.

"What those hens need is layers pellets and perhaps an occasional hot mash. You can't expect eggs if you don't feed them properly," she declared.

From that moment on I started on the rocky path to financial ruin.

The removal of the cocks also set up another problem. For some undoubtedly psychological reason the hens now changed their habits. All of a sudden they stopped straying into the woods and instead started to spend their time on our flower and vegetable beds, scratching up anything which showed signs of growing and making dust baths for themselves where we had expected to produce prize crops of onions, lettuces and carrots.

For a time we contented ourselves with chasing them away but they persisted in returning whenever our backs were turned. And then one morning all was temporarily forgiven when glancing in a nesting box, I saw an egg! A small egg to be sure but an egg nonetheless. Joanna had it for her supper while we all stood around and congratulated each other that all our efforts were at last being rewarded.

This mood of exaltation did not last long. The hens continued to ravage the garden and at the same time started to develop the distinctly anti-social habit of laying their eggs almost anywhere but the nesting boxes which we had so considerately provided. I was constantly coming across nests in odd places like under the summer-house or in the woodshed. One intrepid bird even forgot it was supposed to be a hen to the extent of flying fifteen feet up to the dovecot and laying its eggs there.

It was at this stage that I hit on what seemed to be the ideal solution. We had a large stable building about half a mile from the house and as we had not yet acquired any horses it would seem to be the perfect place to which to banish them.

Nothing to do with the hens was ever as easy as it seemed at first sight and as usual we ran straight away into a snag. We imagined that it would be simple enough to catch them on their perches at night and transport them in the back of the Land Rover to their new home. When, however, we got around to carrying out the operation it was to find that they had given up even that good habit. Instead we discovered to our dismay that they had taken to roosting high up in the surrounding trees.

It was at this stage that my good friend Bob Ballie came to our rescue. Bob is another of those people, like my brothers, who considers himself to be a practical man of action so, when he dropped by one evening and I mentioned my problem to him, he at once volunteered his services.

Unfortunately for him, whilst we waited for it to get sufficiently dark, it came on rain heavily so that when we got to the scene of action, everything was dripping.

Bob however was not to be deterred by a small thing like that. Ladders were fetched and while Diana held the torch we started on the recovery work despite the fact that every step up the ladders brought a fresh shower of cold water down our necks. I was not too badly off as I had a waterproof jacket but Bob, disdaining such mollycoddling, was in his best Sunday suit.

It took hours of swaying about perilously amongst the thin branches before the job was done by which time even Bob was beginning to regret his impetuous offer.

I would like to be able to say at this stage that the hens and I were to live happily ever afterwards. That we did not was entirely due to an act of near lunacy on my part.

To begin with everything went well. The hens no longer ruined the garden and laid dutifully in their new nesting boxes so that we were lulled into a false sense of security. We were getting about a dozen eggs a day and I was beginning to regard my birds with something akin to affection.

It was while in this dangerous state of mind that Diana and I treated ourselves to dinner one night at the Dunkeld House Hotel which had recently been taken over by Gladys Miller and her sister Betty. Formerly the winter house of the Dukes of Atholl they were in the process of turning it into a luxurious hotel, catering for the fastidious tastes of wealthy sportsmen and we had got into the habit of buying ourselves a rich meal there whenever we felt we had something to celebrate.

Talking to Gladys after dinner that night I was boasting about the fine eggs we got, large brown and guaranteed not twenty-four hours old and told her condescendingly that I would be prepared to consider selling her any surplus, to be set of course, against any further gastronomic treats we might have at her hotel. Let us return to the barter system I enthused, envisaging myself living in the future off fresh salmon and fillet steak in return for half a dozen eggs a day.

"Six eggs a day," snorted Gladys, giving me her most scathing look. "If you made it six dozen a day we might do business." She has the knack of putting me down does that Gladys.

Just the same it put ideas into my head. On the way home I discussed it with Diana. If I could sell six dozen a day to one hotel why not others. Why not sixty dozen a day eventually to all the hotels in Dunkeld. Cut out the middleman. No labour to pay. I would do it all myself. Let me see now . . . sixty dozen a day at how much a dozen are they in the shops? I fell asleep in bed that night counting on my fingers.

Next day I went out and bought four hundred pullets.

From that moment my life took on a nightmarish quality. From the beginning those birds wanted for nothing. They took over a stable and two looseboxes. The floors were covered with a thick layer of sawdust and chaff, imported by me with great labour in the Land Rover, the local joiner was contracted to make new and more comfortable nest boxes and the hen food started to arrive by the lorry load.

Anxious that I should bring my flock to full production as soon as possible so as not to miss the summer season with the hotels, I consulted old Peter Campbell who was generally regarded in the district as the final authority on all matters relating to poulty keeping.

Peter was an interesting man. In his long life he had variously been a policeman, patrolling one of the loneliest glens in Scotland on a bicycle, a postman and finally a gamekeeper and man-of-all-work to the son of Sir John Millais the Royal Academician who used to live in the district. It was freely rumoured that when Sir John's son was particularly hard-up, which was quite frequently, he would not pay Peter his salary but would present him instead with a Millais portrait. The walls of his little cottage, it was said, were lined with them.

When we first came to Rohallion Peter was already ninety years old and his wife a year older. They lived only a couple of hundred yards from the end of my drive and, to make a little extra money, Peter had a wooden shed in his garden from which he sold such things as lemonade, sweets and tobacco to passing motorists. He also provided me with my Sunday papers. It was not a satisfactory arrangement. I like to read all the Sundays but the large bundle proved rather too much for Peter. One Sunday I would get two *Observer* colour supplements and no *Times*. Quite frequently I would find that the *News of the World* was from the previous week. If I complained it caused him such anxiety that finally I just accepted what I was given.

Apart from that he was a delightful old man with a fund of stories of the old days so that to make my Sunday morning purchases often took an hour or more. But the real love of his life was hens and on this subject he was inexhaustible. Each week I was regaled with the number of eggs his hens were laying and if it seemed to me that sometimes they must have been producing two eggs each a day I never said anything.

One day I drove Peter up to look at my birds to give his opinion as to their progress.

"If ever there is a nip in the air of a morning," he announced, "you must give them a hot mash. These damned new-fangled pellets are no use at a'."

"That may be all very well if you only have a dozen or so but with over four hundred it will take me all morning to mix the stuff," I protested.

"Are you wanting my advice or are you nae?" he said fixing me with a fierce stare from under his beetling eyebrows.

"And anither thing. Vary their diet. Hens is jist like fowk. They don't want the same thing day after day. No you jist gie them plenty of barley mixed up wi' kibbled maize. Naething like kibbled maize for giving the eggs grand yellow yolks."

I groaned inwardly.

"An' jist a wee pickle o' Karswood spice. That's the greatest thing for bringing them on to the lay."

The hens now started to take me over like John Wyndham's Triffids.

My routine in the morning was to drive the children to school in the village at nine o'clock, pick up Mary and feed the hens on the way home. Where it was once just a matter of chucking out some pellets to them the whole job, what with mixing up a mash and so on, suddenly became much more onerous. It was often well after ten before Mary and I finished the job, our sleeves rolled up to the elbow as we plunged our arms into the soggy mess. Diana started to complain that she was getting no housework done but I was determined to see my hens right.

Then quite suddenly they all started to lay at once. Soon we were getting a hundred eggs a day and then between two and three hundred. Mary and I carried the eggs back to the house in buckets and set them on the kitchen table. Even Diana was impressed.

Presumably those who are in eggs in a big way have elaborate machinery to cope with such chores as washing them, grading them for size and packing them on egg trays. We had no such advantages and washing up to three hundred eggs a day was not only time consuming but exhausting. As for grading them I simply resorted to using an egg cup. If the egg slipped down inside the cup it was discarded as being too small and all the rest whether standard or large were lumped together and sold at the standard price. Nobody was going to complain that I was not giving value for money.

Now that I was getting so many eggs, selling them became a matter of top priority if they were not going to fill the whole kitchen.

Gladys was as good as her word and took well over six dozen a day. To supply Dunkeld House was a pleasure. The head chef was a young man with very civilised ideas of how business should be conducted. When I arrived with his quota of eggs he would invite me into his office to drink a glass of dry sherry while kitchen porters carried in the eggs. Then we would spend a pleasant ten minutes discussing the fishing prospects and other absorbing subjects.

In finding other customers I was not so fortunate. I had hoped to sell my eggs as I did at Dunkeld House, for the price they would have to pay in the shops, relying on the high quality of my eggs and the convenience of having them delivered daily to make it a satisfactory arrangement on both sides. Unfortunately most hoteliers seemed to think that if I was cutting out the middleman, it was they who should reap the financial advantage. Fortunately my brother John, who takes great pride in the excellence of the meals he serves, and Derek Reid at the Tay-bank, came to my rescue but I still had to sell quite a few on the open market.

Then, just as I reached maximum production, the price of eggs started to drop. While the *Daily Mirror* Price Clock recorded increases in other foods week by week, the price of eggs alone fell steadily.

"Just a seasonal decrease," my mother said comfortingly. "You'll have to take the rough with the smooth." When eggs finally hit a new low I had a polite circular from my suppliers saying that they were forced to put up the price of hen food. I put the ciruclar in the wastepaper basket and gritted my teeth. As my literary output became more and more spasmodic, the hens increased their hold over my life.

With the cutting of the crops in the autumn a new hazard arose. Each day when I went down to collect the eggs I began to notice more and more empty eggshells lying about in the nesting boxes. I feared that the hens must be eating their own eggs. This is a well-known bad habit of hens and one which is very difficult to cure.

Mary was the first one to give me a clue that this might not be the problem. Some of the hens had perversely taken to laying in the loft above the stables which can only be reached through a narrow chute which used to be used to fork down the hay stored above for the horses. Because Mary has a rather more athletic figure than mine it was she who usually had the job of retrieving them. With her skirt hitched up above her knees she would clamber through the hole and hand the eggs down to me.

One morning as she raised her head through the hole she saw several enormous rats scampering across the floor and a tell-tale number of empty eggshells.

"Of course it's the rats," Peter said when I put the matter to him. "They aye come into the buildings at the end of the harvest looking for easy feeding."

"But how on earth does a rat break a hen's egg?" I asked. "I mean you'd hardly think their teeth would be large enough."

"Oh, they manage that easy enough. But that is not the worst of it. They take more eggs down into their holes than they eat outside." Then he started on one of his wonderful stories.

"I mind well when I was a wee laddie, seeing how the rats do it. I was standing quietly in my father's barn one day when I saw two rats come out of their hole. Well I niver let on that I was there but just watched them. One of the rats rolls an egg out of a hen's nest and turns over on its back holding the egg between its forefeet. Then the other rat grabs it by the tail and pulls it and the egg down the rathole. Would you believe such a thing?"

"I would not, Peter Campbell," I said. "And it's a damned liar you are!"

"Please yoursel' whether you believe me or not but I'm telling you I saw it with my own eyes."

Whatever the truth of Peter's story I had a real rat problem. Next day I bought a large tin of Warfarin and spread it liberally around the rat holes. The following morning it was all gone and within forty-eight hours I had picked up over a hundred dead rats.

So Mary and I soldiered on through the winter, breaking the ice so that the hens could have water and trying to keep up their morale with hot mashes. In spite of anything we could do, however, the daily collection produced fewer and fewer eggs while the price in the open market remained stubbornly low.

With the coming of spring matters started to improve until the hens took it into their heads to start brooding. Every day there were more and more hens, stubbornly sitting on an empty nest and refusing to move. I was furious at this new development feeling it to be an act of the basest treachery after all the care I had lavished on them during the winter. When the gamekeeper from up the glen called in to see if I had any hens under which he could hatch out his pheasant chicks, I gladly got rid of a couple of dozen 'broodies'. This was really the beginning of the end.

There was a short time in the early summer when production once again soared almost to the level of the previous year but it soon fell away as more and more of the idiotic creatures started to moult.

Finally, with the prospect of another winter ahead I rang up the poultry dealer in Perth and offered him the lot at a give-away price if he could come and collect them.

When I came to work out my profit and loss account I discovered that I had lost about 10p on every hen for each month that I had kept them.

7

For me one of the great delights of Rohallion was the loch. After so many years in the South where any form of sport is so ridiculously expensive and difficult to come by it was wonderful to feel that I could pick up a rod any time and stroll down to the waterside.

In fact the loch is so surrounded by rhododendrons that there are only two places where you can fish from the bank. Taking the boat out added to my pleasure. Sometimes when my writing was not going as it should I would get into the boat and let it drift where the breeze took it simply for the intense pleasure it gave me. Lying in the stern with my feet propped up on the seat, I would lie back and watch the slowly drifting clouds and the birds which every now and again flew across my field of vision. Often there would be a pair of hawks circling high in the sky, their wings scarcely seeming to move; busy little teal and the more ponderous mallard would appear suddenly and splash into the water, heedless of the boat, and the wood pigeons would salute each other from tree to tree. I would return after an hour or so refreshed in spirit and sit down at the typewriter again with renewed energy.

For the most part, however, it was the rising trout which I found irresistible. When we first moved in I had taken over the morning room as my study and placed my desk in the bow window which overlooked the water. The distractions, however, proved too great. Gazing out of the window, seeking inspiration, my eye would catch the movement of deer across the hillside and out would come my field glasses. Then a particular trout would attract my notice, rising regularly within easy reach of the bank until I had to go down and cast a fly over it.

In the end I gave up the uneven struggle and moved my typewriter into a room on the other side of the house in order to get any work done at all.

The trout in the loch are not large. To catch one of a pound is a matter for celebration but they are extremely lively so that every time you hook one you get the momentary thrill that this is going to be the big one. They are also wonderful eating, with pinkish flesh and as sweet as a nut. When conditions are right there is no difficulty in catching a dozen or so in a couple of hours but I usually restrict myself to catching just enough for a meal for the family.

The only art is to position the boat in just the right place so that it drifts within casting distance of the side. Then you can drop your flies as close into the rhododendron bushes as you can where the bigger ones are waiting for natural flies to fall into the water. When you hook one you have to be quick for instinctively it will try to dive back under the branches which overhang the water by three or four feet. If you let him get away with this manoeuvre you will be likely to finish up in a dreadful tangle. All in all it just requires enough concentration to keep your mind fully absorbed.

It was not long before I discovered that there were other fish besides brown trout in the loch. Every now and again I would hook a little perch and it soon became apparent that they were there in considerable numbers.

I am not particularly fond of perch. They have spiky fins which can cut your hand and they are full of bones which make them difficult to eat. Moreover I felt rather resentful that they were eating food which the trout could have had and which might result in them growing to a bigger size.

For all these reasons I decided to invest in some perch traps and try to reduce the population. The perch trap would at first sight seem to be the most idiotic way ever devised for catching fish. It is made entirely of wire and is about three feet long by two feet high. The only entry is by a funnel shaped hole at one end of the trap. It is through this that the fish are supposed to squeeze themselves and, once in, the narrowness of the end of the funnel makes it difficult if not impossible for them to get out again. Why they should want to squeeze their way in in the first place is a mystery to me, for no bait of any sort is put inside the trap to attract them. The contraption is simply tied to a long piece of rope which in turn is attached to a small marker buoy and lowered to the bottom of the loch.

The answer to this improbable proposition is, I gather, that the perch find it an attractive place to spawn and once one or two are inside the rest follow.

Whatever the reason for their fascination, the traps were an amazing success. I took Charlie with me when we went out for the first time to haul them up and we both nearly fell out of the boat with surprise. The first trap was so packed with fish that there would scarcely have been room for another one. And so it was with each trap we pulled up. Occasionally an eel would find its way in with the perch but there were never any trout. They were too smart.

In spite of my remaining aloof from John Bennett's eel cooking experiment, I have always been fascinated by eels and their strange life cycle which I described in *Against the Wind*. My younger brother, John, has an eel trap on the stream which joins the chain of lochs stretching down the valley from Dunkeld. In the autumn when they start their final journey back to the Sargasso Sea he catches them in considerable quantities and sends them off live to Billingsgate.

On one occasion when I pulled up a perch trap I discovered two eels inside apparently stuck together. On closer examination I found that one eel, only marginally the larger of the two, was trying to swallow the other and already had drawn it well down its throat. I pulled them apart and the eel which was in the process of being devoured wriggled off quite happily but I believe if I had left them to it, the cannibal would have succeeded in the almost impossible task of swallowing its mate. I wonder how many easily swallowed small fish they account for.

In time the number of perch I caught in my traps started to diminish. I do not believe that this was because I had made any considerable impression on their numbers but simply that the breeding season was almost over. Eventually I was only pulling up the traps every two or three days and was just thinking of giving them up altogether when one morning I made the most extraordinary catch.

Pulling up one trap it felt so heavy that for a moment I thought it had got entangled with a sunken branch. When I brought it to the surface however it was to discover that it was full of twenty or thirty very large tench.

Now tench are not very common fish in Scotland and particularly as far north as Perthshire. They are more normally to be found in English ponds and in the midland canals so beloved by the great army of coarse fishermen. I felt much more attracted to tench than to perch. I don't know whether it is my imagination but their eyes seem to be less cold and glassy than those of other fish. They have an almost melancholy look and their absurdly small pursed mouths have a feminine appeal. If nothing else, their delightful Latin name of *Tinca Tinca* would predispose me in their favour.

I feel too that they have nice natures. They are sometimes known as the 'doctor fish' because if they find another fish which is ailing they will swim alongside and rub themselves against the invalid and it is said that their scales are covered with slime which has peculiar curative properties. They are also bottom feeders, nosing about for their food in the mud which in turn drives the gamer fish to seek their food on the surface and so make them easier to catch for the fly fisherman. In the winter they bury themselves in the mud completely and only come out of hibernation when the warmer weather returns.

That bright Spring morning when I pulled up the trap full of tench I was unwilling to kill such fine looking fish for no reason. At the same time I felt that one or two of them might provide an acceptable meal. Did not the monks of old stock their ponds with tench and carp for that very purpose? Accordingly I released most of the prisoners and leaving half a dozen still in the trap, rowed ashore to consult Diana's library of cookery books.

One old book, rather contemptuously I thought, recommended them as suitable for making fish cakes, but Mrs. Beeton as usual had the last word on the subject. She came up with no less than three recipes. According to her they could either be baked and served with a white sauce or marinaded and grilled or finally served as an elaborate dish which required amongst other ingredients, a dozen oysters.

Diana was enthusiastic about this sudden piscatorial windfall. We had our near neighbours, Peter and Anne Stock coming for supper and here was a wonderful opportunity to save on the housekeeping money whilst at the same time producing something really rather special.

I did not go out to pick up the fish until after five o'clock that afternoon, but when I came to pull up the trap it was quite empty. At first it seemed to be quite inexplicable. The tench each weighed almost two pounds and I had thought it remarkable that they had been able to squeeze into the trap in the first place. To make the return journey down the funnel would have been quite impossible.

It was then that I noticed that the wire on the back wall of the trap had been cut through as if with wire-cutters so that when I pushed a gaping hole appeared through which my fish had undoubtedly escaped. It was a feat beyond the capabilities of the most voracious of fish. That the soft, sucking lips of the tench should conceal such razor sharp teeth seemed to me incredible.

Perversely I felt they had let me down rather badly in not allowing themselves to be made into an easy supper, a feeling which was not in any way lessened by the fact that it was too late to get anything from the shops and I was stuck with taking the household out to dinner.

There was an amusing sequel to the discovery of the tench. One summer morning I was about to set out reluctantly for Perth when a car drove up from which there emerged three men whom I had never seen before. I peered at them cautiously through the drawing room window, fearful that they might have come to cut off the electricity or impound my furniture. This fear I have is very real. Not only have I all my life been short of money but, even when there is something in the Bank, I have the sort of mind which can conveniently forget that items like electricity, telephone, rates and even the rent are long overdue. I have come to regard the arrival of strange men therefore with some trepidation.

On this occasion, however, it was obvious that the visitors were much more interested in the loch than they were in the house. They stared at it intently, every now and again shaking their heads dolefully.

When I went out to see what they wanted, it was to learn that they had spent the previous evening at my brother's hotel and my sister-in-law, Annette, had told them about the tench.

They were dedicated coarse fishermen and had driven up from the Midlands to see what sort of sport Scotland might have to offer.

"I'm afraid there has been some mistake," one of them said apologetically. "This is obviously not tench water. Sorry to have bothered you."

"We thought it was too good to be true – tench in a Scottish loch," another of them said sadly.

"That's just where you are wrong," I said, feeling rather put on my mettle. "There's plenty of tench there – if you can catch them."

They still looked rather dubious but, on my insisting that they had a go, they started to unload their equipment from their large motor car whilst I watched fascinated. From metal cases which looked as if they ought to have contained half a dozen billiard cues, they produced rods which when put together seemed to me to be of enormous length. There followed baskets and keep nets, stools and rod rests with a multitude of floats and boxes, lines and reels and picnic baskets.

Although I was already late for my appointment, I could not resist waiting to watch them setting it all up. When all was ready a large cake tin was produced which, when opened, turned out to be full to the brim with several pounds of writhing maggots which they threw in great handfuls into the water.

At this point, apologising for the shortage of fishing space on the bank, I had to leave.

Later in the day, when I returned, I found the three of them looking as radiant as if they had won the football pools. Their keep nets, tethered to the bank, bulged to bursting point with tench and every few minutes one or other of their rods would start to vibrate violently as they pulled in yet another fish.

By the time they came to leave they had over seventy and were wearing looks of stunned disbelief. Finally all the fish were tipped out onto the bank and they had their photographs taken standing proudly by their catch. Then to my surprise they threw them all back into the water.

"The photographs are all we want," they explained. "Our mates will never believe us unless we have the evidence."

"Well," I said, "if any of your mates want to come up and have a go I'd be only too pleased."

All three of them looked at me with an astonishment which was tinged with horror.

"What!" One of them exclaimed. "Let some of our pals into the secret. We'd have to be mad! This place is worth a king's ransom to us. If we could find fishing like this where we live it would cost us hundreds of pounds."

That Christmas we received a card showing a picture of the catch and signed, "Your three fishing friends."

They have been back every year since but alas, the great success of that first visit has not been repeated and although I look forward to their annual visit, I have never yet got to know their names.

It is said that there are many more people who go fishing every Saturday than turn out to watch football matches which gives my faith in human nature a boost. Surely nothing can be more revivifying than a few hours spent by the water side engrossed in the gentle art. Of course there are many people for whom fishing has no appeal. "I don't have the patience for it," they usually say but fishing is not a matter of patience.

Although the days when one returns home triumphant with a basket full of fish are red letter ones, the blank days also have their charm. Water has a unique fascination not only in itself but in the life it supports. Just to sit on a river bank and watch the business of living going on around one is to relax in mind and body and banish the pressures which beset us all from time to time.

Of the great body of fishermen in these islands the majority restrict themselves either by choice or necessity to coarse fishing. They above all others must love fishing for its own sake for they seldom seem to have the urge to keep what they catch. They do not have the hunter instinct of the rest of us to return with a trophy to establish our prowess in the eyes of others. Instead they content themselves with recording the weight of their catch before returning it to the water. Nothing in the world would induce me to throw back a fine trout and when it comes to salmon fishing there is the added incentive that you can nowadays sell your salmon for over a pound sterling per pound avoirdupois.

All of which makes my American cousin by marriage a very remarkable fisherman indeed. I first met him a year or so after

64

we had moved into Rohallion when he and my cousin announced that they had arrived unexpectedly at Gleneagles Hotel at the start of a prolonged tour of Scotland.

From the magnificence of their suite at that far from inexpensive hostelry and the list of hotels on their itinerary I deduced that my new found cousin must not only be a very rich man indeed but a dedicated golfer. When I put the matter to him however he looked at me in amazement.

"Golf!" he exclaimed. "Why if you gave me a golf club I wouldn't know whether to shove it up my nose or stick it in my ear."

"Then why St. Andrews and Turnberry and Nairn," I asked bewildered.

"Royal is a dedicated fisherman," my cousin Nell explained. "He's fished everywhere in the world from Iceland to New Zealand. Finally he's got around to Scotland."

I should explain here that his first name is Royal which is confusing enough without his surname which happens to be Knight.

Now I had to tell them as gently as I could that their New York agents had boobed. They had booked them into half a dozen hotels which, apart from all being expensive, had in common the finest golf courses Scotland had to offer as well as being as far as possible from any good fishing rivers.

When this dawned on Royal Knight I thought he was going to burst a blood vessel.

After a great deal of anxious telephoning I managed to salvage something out of the mess. Next day they moved out of Gleneagles. By a stroke of luck I got them into Balathie House Hotel, one of the finest fishing hotels on the Tay and better still achieved a boat on one of the better beats.

That night I sought out Willie Laird, a prince among gillies. He is a little brown nut of a man with a thirst to suit a man twice his size. When he laughs which is frequently it comes out like the noises of bathwater going down the plug hole.

I took him to the Branch Office and explained to him all about Royal Knight being one of the finest handlers of a rod in America and a fisherman of international repute.

"The are a' the same tae me," said Willie, unimpressed, but he was soon to change his tune.

65

Royal arrived on the water, punctual to the minute in an enormous limousine which had once done service for the President of the United States. It was however when he started to assemble his equipment that Willie realised that he had a far from run of the mill customer.

Most of the visitors who come to fish the Tay use spinning rods. Not for them the more delicate technique of the fly fishermen. They are content to sit in a boat with their bait trolling out of the stern whilst the gillie draws it across the most likely lies. In most cases it is the gillie's skill which hooks the fish and all the customer has to do is to land it.

Royal Knight would have none of this. He will only fish with a fly and uses a rod so light that Willie thought at first that he was after trout. He was indeed a remarkable fisherman and it was not long before he hooked his first fish. Willie watched anxiously as the little rod bent almost double but eventually it was safely in the net, a nice clean-run fish of about twelve pounds. Royal took one look at it and grunted.

"Throw it back," he said. Willie was so surprised that he almost fell out of the boat. In all his experience he had never known anyone return a good fish to the water.

"I only keep specimen fish of thirty pounds or over," Royal explained.

They landed several more that day but none of them came up to the exacting standards required. That evening when I dropped in to see how Willie had got on I found a very frustrated gillie indeed.

"Can ye imagine it?" he gasped, looking very like a landed salmon himself, "Straight back into the river. I could have wept."

The next morning the big limousine arrived again exactly on time but this time there was no Royal. He had caught a heavy cold and had been ordered to bed. Willie was to fish the river himself and ask anyone he liked as Mr. Knight's guests, the chauffeur told him. As it happened Willie had another good day and this time the catch was brought safely home. Royal never got back to the Tay but he paid up cheerfully.

"He was a wee topper o' a man," Willie said to me sometime afterwards, adding, "even if he was a bit saft in the heid."

Salmon fishing has its moments of high excitement but, to my mind, it does not compare with the joys of fishing for trout. The very names of the flies one uses are magic – Grouse and Claret, Bloody Butcher, March Brown and Hare's Lug. My own favourite which, I sometimes feel, gives me an almost unfair advantage over those who do not know it, is called a Grey Monkey. Few fishing tackle dealers have even heard of it. I was first given one by the Rohallion postman soon after I arrived – a truly unselfish act for fishermen like to preserve their own secrets – and I have hooked fish with it all over Scotland when my companions are returning with empty baskets.

Scotland is, of course, a fisherman's paradise and I was not slow to take advantage of it. Apart from being one of the great salmon rivers, the Tay holds some wonderful trout. As the days grow warmer bringing out hatches of flies on the Dunkeld House water, there are picnics by the waterside and during the summer we make long expeditions into the hills, bouncing over the boulder strewn tracks to spend the day on some remote moorland loch while my typewriter stands reproachfully silent on my desk.

Dedicated trout fisherman I may be but it in no way lessens my sympathy for Snowy who is the gillie on the beat below Dunkeld. Fishing for salmon on his own from a boat he hooked a fish so monstrous that he had it on for three hours before it finally broke free. By that time it had towed him four miles downstream. I have borne my own small fishing tragedies with courage but I think if I had been Snowy I would have wept.

8

ONE OF our early worries was whether the children would fit into the village school where we intended to send them. Fiona was already twelve and was to be pitchforked into a typical Scottish day school which could hardly be in greater contrast to her experience of a school run by Maltese nuns. To a lesser extent Neil and Charlie had to make the transition from an English day school with its different curriculum and standards of discipline. Even their having 'English' accents we feared might make them stand out as being different for to be different is not always a desirable thing during one's schooldays. Only Jo-Jo was young enough not to have any problems. When her turn eventually came she soon became so Scottish in her speech that we were hard put to understand some of the things she said.

The Dunkeld School however we were soon to discover had an individuality of its own. It had been granted the right to be called the Royal School of Dunkeld in perpetuity by King James VI of Scotland who had founded it in 1562, a date which makes it a near contemporary of that rather more distinguished grammar school, Eton. In those days the fees were 2/6 a quarter. It is now free. A fine example of deflation.

Since its earliest days it has been under the patronage of the Atholl family and the houses into which it is divided bear the family names of Atholl, Stewart and Murray. The school song is sung in Gaelic and Gaelic is still one of the subjects in the curriculum.

We need not in fact have worried about our lot. They not only integrated without any difficulty but their standard of work rapidly improved. They would come back with lurid tales of who had had 'the belt' and for what dreadful misdemeanours, for

68

corporal punishment is still kept on as the final deterrent but they themselves successfully managed to avoid it.

The traditions of the school and the cathedral have a big influence on the inhabitants of the City of Dunkeld – never let them hear you referring to it as a village – and they are proud of their traditions. The graveyards of both the Cathedral and the Church of Little Dunkeld on the other side of the river are the last resting places of many famous names.

No less a fearsome figure than Alister More Mac an Righ, third son of King Robert III and better known to history as the Wolf of Badenoch lies in the vestibule to the Cathedral choir. It seems to me he was lucky to be given a Christian burial. A notorious marauder, he spent much of his turbulent life plundering church lands and on one occasion burnt the cathedral at Elgin to the ground. His father made him do penance for his sins but it did not make him alter his ways.

Close to the Wolf's memorial lies the grandson of Bonnie Prince Charlie. His life was less heroic. He was killed when the Royal Mail coach overturned at nearby Inver. An early victim of dangerous driving.

The churchyard at Little Dunkeld is filled with local worthies, some of whose reputations spread far beyond the confines of their parish. One of them is Neil Gow, the most famous fiddler ever to come out of Scotland.

Gow lived at Inver where Robert Burns met him in 1787. He described him in his diary as 'a short, stout-built, Highland figure with greyish hair shed on his honest social brow.' His expertness with the fiddle was quite remarkable in a country where the fiddle overshadows even the bagpipes as the national instrument.

It was said of Gow that he was the owner of a cow which was almost as remarkable as its master. It was Gow's habit to sit under a large oak tree on the banks of the Tay playing his music to anyone who cared to listen. It was his cow which did the work. It was in the days before there was a bridge and farmers used to swim their reluctant cattle across the river just below where Gow sat. On receiving a small payment Gow would order his cow into the river to encourage the others across. Its duty completed it would then swim back to its master.

Although all the Gow family had taken part in the '45

Rebellion it was overlooked sufficiently for him to be commanded to play before the English Court only a few years later. He died in 1807, when it was written:

"Gow and times are even now.
Gow beat time, now time's beat Gow."

Another outstanding local character who also lived at Inver was Charles Mackintosh, the naturalist. He started work as a boy with the sawmill which was still at Inver when we came to Rohallion. In an unfortunate accident he lost his thumb but it was a blessing in disguise. He took employment as a postman walking twenty miles a day six days a week and it was during his walks that his interest in natural history was fostered. He discovered many new species and was an expert in tree diseases. Although his reputation spread far afield he himself never left his own beloved countryside. He was honoured by being elected President of the Perthshire Natural Science Society and when he died in 1922 he bequeathed his collection of specimens to the City of Perth where it attracts botanists to this day.

This may be a not inappropriate place to relate a little more of the history of the place where we had come to live as I heard it bit by bit from the older inhabitants.

Ever since its beginnings as a religious centre Dunkeld has been a prosperous little community. The Danes thought it worth plundering and rowed their long boats up the Tay in 724 to sack the village – a feat which must cause some wonder to the canoe club who negotiate the turbulent waters downstream from Dunkeld Bridge to Perth in their annual race.

In 850 Kenneth MacAlpin made Dunkeld his capital so that it was briefly the most important place in Scotland but on the whole it has preferred to sleep on undisturbed. There must have been a flurry of excitement when in 1745 Cameron of Lochiel stood by the Old Cross and declared Charles Stuart to be the rightful King but a year later Dunkeld found itself in the role of advance headquarters for 'Butcher' Cumberland's avenging army on their way to the final confrontation at Culloden.

It was about the time of the '45 Rebellion that the flax trade started to develop. By the end of the century the fields were blue with the flax flower and there was a lively cottage weaving industry. The village was also a centre for the tanning industry.

There was plenty of casual work stripping the bark off the oak trees for the tanners and the finished boots and shoes were sent all over Scotland. There were slate quarries on the hills above Birnam and Caputh and even a sideline in pearl fishing in the Tay where the fresh water mussel flourishes.

By the middle of the nineteenth century, however, flax had become big business and had moved out of the cottages into big mills in places like Montrose. If you take a walk up Strathbraan you will come across groups of cottages lying forlorn and empty where in about 1850 whole communities gave up the struggle and migrated together to Canada and America.

The leather trade too ceased to be a cottage industry. Mass production methods were introduced with which they could not compete and one by one the individual craftsmen were forced out of business. Even the slate quarries closed and the pearls grew fewer.

Finally after its own little industrial revolution Dunkeld reverted to an agricultural community supporting a weekly cattle market and six large annual fairs.

Despite the fact that at the very height of its prosperity Dunkeld never had a population of more than 1,500 and usually nearer 1,000 it was still a prosperous enough community to support three Banks and there were few insurance companies who did not have a resident representative competing for the local business.

The building of the bridge was an event which had a far reaching effect. It opened up Dunkeld as a stopping place on the journey to the north and led to its establishment as a tourist centre.

As with most things to do with 'the city' the Duke of Atholl of the day played a prominent part. The local inhabitants subscribed about £5,500 and the Duke of that time put up the balance of over £20,000 in return for which he was entitled to exact a toll. It was a shrewd move on his part. Not only did it help to open up the whole of the Highlands but it brought a new prosperity in particular to his own estate of over 200,000 acres which lay to the north of the river.

The toll levied was a halfpenny a head and an idea of the use made of the bridge may be gained from the fact that even at this low rate, the income produced was between £800 and £900 a year.

I have been told repeatedly by locals whose great grandparents could have been at the opening that the bridge was actually built on dry land, the Tay being diverted from its course for the purpose. I find this hard to believe but when I express my doubts I am shouted down by people like Peter the Provost who might have been there himself from the way he sets himself up as an authority on the matter. What is certain is that just after the bridge was built the local prison was closed down and for many years one of the arches on the Birnam side which is on dry land was closed in and used for the purpose. It is also certain that the bridge just over a hundred years ago precipitated a major crisis in village affairs.

It all came about because a local coal merchant who had much occasion to use the bridge decided that it was time the toll was abolished. He worked out that the Dukes of Atholl had long been amply repaid for their munificence and should not be allowed to continue to exact their toll.

Alexander Robertson, 'The Dundonnachie' as he was known locally, was of the stuff which village Hamptons are made. It took considerable courage in those days to stand up against the omnipotence of the Lairds and particularly so powerful a laird as the Duke of Atholl. After all had he not just had Queen Victoria herself staying at his castle?

Robertson was, however, certain of the justice of his cause and mounted a vigorous campaign. First he refused to pay the tolls himself, driving his cart past the toll gate and abusing the gatekeeper to such an extent that he complained to the Duke.

Soon there were others who rallied to the banner of the Dundonnachie. When the Duke threatened them with the law they replied by tearing down the wooden toll gates and throwing them into the river. The Duke retaliated by having iron gates erected but Sandy Robertson was a powerful man. Arming himself with an axe he hacked the gates to pieces and sold the bars to a local blacksmith for 5/6 each.

Finding that local sympathy was growing on the side of the rebels the Duke bypassed the police and called out the army to defend his property. Even he, however, could not retain the services of the army for ever and as soon as they withdrew the campaign started again.

Over the years Robertson reduced himself to poverty in his

fight against the tolls and made many powerful enemies but in the end he won the day. After eleven years, on 15th May 1879, the County finally took over the bridge and abolished the toll.

Lawlessness was however alien to the nature of the villagers. The main crime was nothing more cardinal than swearing with occasional cases of drunkenness and the prison under the bridge was seldom used. The most powerful figure in the community, after the Duke himself, was the minister.

Beatrix Potter, who used to come to Dunkeld on holiday with her parents every year and kept a secret diary in code which has only recently been deciphered (by Leslie Linder), has left many amusing reminiscences of her visits. One concerns the Cathedral minister conducting a service. In 1892 she wrote:

"The portion of the cathedral where public worship is held is walled out of the old building in an ugly arbitrary fashion. It is very plain inside and down below intensely cold. We generally sit in the west gallery, the high old pews distressingly covered with heiroglyphics. They are open under the seat and non non quam descends a peppermint hop, hop from tier to tier . . ."

Mr. Rutherford, the minister was ". . . earnest, pale and foxy haired with a pointed beard and decent Geneva bands. Perched just below him (the pulpit is very high) is the Precentor, a fair big man with a bullet head, chubby red face, retroussé nose and a voice like a bull. He is the Birnam schoolmaster. He pitches all the tunes too high and it seems etiquette that he begins a note before the congregation and prolongs the last note after them in a long buzz."

The Potter family took several houses over a long period of years in the district. Their main house had been Dalguise up the river but when that ceased to be available they took a pretty rambling house above the railway station, known as The Lodge.

At some stage, however, the Potters must have taken Eastwood, another lovely house on the Tay where our Royal Family often come to stay, for it is in a letter dated 1893 from Eastwood that Beatrix writes to the son of a former governess. It starts:

73

"My dear Noel,

I don't know what to write you so I shall tell you a story about four little rabbits whose names were Flopsy, Mopsy, Cottontail and Peter . . ."

Beatrix Potter also commented on the arrival of Bostock and Wombwell's Circus which must have been a considerable occasion. She herself found it delightful but . . . "The only single animal which looked out of sorts or unhappy was one of a pair of performing elephants who was deplorably ill with a cold. Her keeper, a big black-haired fellow seemed much concerned and invited her 'Nancy, poor old girl,' to share his supper but she dropped it and stood with her trunk crumpled up on the bar like a sick worm. The poor thing died three days later at Coupar Angus . . ."

When the railway first came to Dunkeld in 1836 it was the furthest point it extended into the highlands which gave travellers a sense of adventure. Even before that the place had a reputation as a health resort and indeed there was a local club known as the 84 Club which only admitted members over that age. These factors coupled with the fine sport to be had in the district tempted a speculator to build a grandiose hotel between the river and the railway. It still stands today, an extraordinary edifice in the Scottish baronial fashion of the times with great wrought iron gates leading to nowhere, a banqueting hall and bedrooms the size of billiards saloons and bathrooms to match.

It was purpose built to provide suitable accommodation for the increasing numbers of grandees who, following in the steps of Queen Victoria were discovering the Highlands and for a time it succeeded in its purpose. The Spanish Royal Family came to stay there year after year and many other important person-ages besides. It was in fact the Gleneagles of the nineteenth century and has carried vestiges of its former glory into the twentieth. I pass it each morning on my way to pick up Mary and always look to see how many Rolls Royces are parked outside the front door. It is a disappointing morning when there are not any.

If the visitor to Rohallion is not minded to take the main road in his motor car and has the time and energy to spend he can take the footpath out of Birnam which runs up behind the railway station and climb to the shoulder of Birnam Hill from where he can look down on the great vista of the Tay Valley on one side and the spires of Rohallion on the other. If he has any puff left he can leave the track and make the final almost vertical climb to the crest.

This rather inaccessible terrain must have had some special significance in the time of pre-history for, if you can find them amongst the tall bracken, there are a cluster of what are known to archaeologists as 'cup stones'.

Cup stones are just that. Large stones set in the ground with a hollowed out cup on the top. The cups are obviously man-made but how this was done is as hard to conjecture as it is to discover a purpose. It is generally considered that they must have had some religious significance but for what manner of people no one can hazard a guess.

Alongside the cup stones and of much more recent if no less obscure origin there are the remains of a small fort, described rather misleadingly on the Ordnance Survey map as Rohallion Castle. Every summer we have people coming to the door at Rohallion asking to be directed to the 'castle', who are disappointed when they are told that it is little more than an outline of thick stone walls standing at the highest at not more than four feet.

There are many theories as to why someone should have gone to the trouble of fortifying a mountain top on the road to nowhere. Did a drove road once go over the hill and the fort serve as a toll booth or was it once the refuge of some local marauder who retired there with his plunder? Nobody seems to know, not even Dick Stewart, our local historian who spends much of his time trying to reconstruct it.

Whatever the origin of these two relics of the past they provide a great deal of entertainment for Charlie. When we have guests up from the south who feel that a mild stroll might do good to their constitutions, Charlie asks them with wide-eyed innocence if they would like to visit the castle. "It's just over there," he says pointing vaguely in the direction of Allen's Bridge.

On their enthusiastic agreement he starts off with them along the wide timber road which runs through the pine woods until they get to a criss-cross of paths which we have christened Piccadilly Circus.

"Which way now?" they ask surveying the several easy routes which lead downhill.

"Up there," says Charlie, pointing to the perpendicular hill which rises above them . . . Usually their vanity will not allow them to turn back at this stage and we are accustomed to very pink and exhausted guests returning some hours later.

9

It was during the third Spring we spent at Rohallion that it became obvious even to me that we were facing a severe financial crisis.

As authors, who insist none the less on being authors – and what else can they do poor souls – are quick to tell everyone, writing is not a very secure way of life. Certainly there are a few who make vast sums of money and retire to tax free havens to enjoy their spoils but they are much more rare than big winners on the football pools. The rest of us jog along philosophically taking the rough with the smooth, hoping that the next book will be the big one.

One of the hardships of an author's life is that he has no nice comfortable monthly pay packet. His pay days only come twice a year and then it is for books sold perhaps nine months earlier. In the meantime the demands of the electricity and telephone people, the rating authorities and the landlord wait for no man. The butcher, the baker and the candlestick maker can go to the lending library and enjoy his books free but they do not extend to him similar facilities when it comes to bread, meat or even candlesticks.

I'm not really complaining, for an author's life has many other compensations, but only explaining that financial crises are not an unfamiliar feature of my life. This Spring, however, the financial hangover of our move from the South had made the situation even more critical than usual. Buff envelopes poured through the letter box in a never-ending stream and from the noises being made by the Electricity Board it looked as if any moment we might be plunged into darkness. Even I, who as I have already said, normally have the happy facility of being able to put such irritations to the back of my mind realised that something would have to be done – but what?

More to convince myself that I was doing something than for any other reason I called a family conference. It was rather like shutting the stable door after the horse has gone but I read everybody a lecture on the necessity of economy. Lights must be switched off, electric fires not left burning in bedrooms and water was just as refreshing as milk or orange squash. By and large they listened with attention except for Jo-Jo who kept turning somersaults in the middle of the floor, interrupting my flow of rhetoric when I had to stop to admonish her.

I thought I had made my point pretty well about the need for stringent economy but I was unprepared for the children's reaction.

Two days later on the Friday of the Spring Bank Holiday weekend, Fiona headed a deputation which had an important matter to discuss. Fiona, unlike the others is a very quiet withdrawn person not much given to small talk but when she has something to say one might as well try to dam the Tay as stop her.

This was one of those occasions.

"About what you were saying about not having any money," she started, "well we have been talking it over and we have had this terrific idea."

"Go on," I said encouragingly.

"You know all the daffodils we have. There are daffodils everywhere. I mean down by the stables there are literally *seas* of daffodils. Now with tomorrow being the Saturday of the Bank Holiday weekend we will hardly be able to get out of our gates for cars passing and most of them will be people from the towns who may not have any daffodils of their own."

"What we plan to do is to get up very early tomorrow morning and pick masses and masses and have a little stall at the end of the drive and sell them."

"Then we could give you the money and you would not have to worry any more," said Jo-Jo.

I must say that I was very touched.

The daffodils at Rohallion are indeed splendid. They grow everywhere, lining the avenue and exploding into great clumps in clearings in the woods and down by the stream which

78

runs past the stables. They are of every variety from the pale almost transparent-petalled ones to those with deep rich yellow trumpets.

Next morning the children were up at first light, chattering like starlings with excitement.

"I bet we make a hundred pounds," said Jo-Jo, that being the largest sum of money she could imagine.

"Even if we make five pounds Daddy will be pleased," said Charlie more practically.

Every bucket was commandeered and a big tin bath to be used for the reserve supplies. There were piles of newspapers so that each customer could have their purchase gift wrapped while Neil, the craftsman in the family had created a huge cardboard sign nailed to a pole which bore the inscription:

DAFFS FOR
SALE 1/6

Bearing this before them like a crusader's banner they set off in the highest of good spirits.

It turned out to be a scorching day. By mid-morning Diana and I thought we would demonstrate our support by taking them down a bottle of lemonade.

We found four rather despondent little figures sitting behind their improvised table which still groaned with the weight of buckets of daffodils. Nobody had stopped to buy at all.

"One woman *nearly* bought some," said Charlie, making the best of it.

"There was a hold up in the traffic and we saw her reach for her handbag but then the traffic moved on too soon."

"The trouble is that there is too much traffic," said Neil. "Nobody can stop with a lot of cars behind them."

"Perhaps they are too expensive," suggested Fiona. "I think we should cut our price. After all they did not cost us anything in the first place."

This was generally agreed and we left them busily altering the sign, advertising a dramatic reduction to three pence a bunch.

Lunch time came and went. Determined not to miss a possible sale they came up to the house in relays to eat. By teatime the price had been cut to a penny a bunch and the procession of cars

79

had been reduced to a trickle. The sun was dropping behind Rohallion Hill before they gave up. Still no one had stopped.

It was a sad end to a brave effort. They insisted in all coming with me in the Land Rover to deliver the flowers to the local hospital and on the way back we went round by Dunkeld to stop at Roberto's and buy fish and chips.

By the time we got home again they had quite recovered their spirits. Children are very resilient over life's little tragedies.

*   *   *

Not even the ominous noises being made by our creditors could spoil for us the glories of that spring. The previous year we had been too preoccupied with the business of settling into our house and entertaining visitors to enjoy the full beauty of the season. Now each week seemed to bring a fresh delight. As the days started to lengthen and the water grew warmer the trout started to rise and the birds like the swallows, the house martins and the green plover returned from their long winter migrations.

One night, shortly after Diana and I had retired to bed we were awakened out of a half sleep by what sounded like low voices outside our window.

"It is some people trying to break in," Diana whispered, agitatedly shaking me into full wakefulness.

"Nonsense," I grumbled, thinking of all those cartoon situations which humourists so enjoy depicting the shivering man of the house in his nightshirt confronting a formidable-looking burglar.

The murmuring however grew louder and louder and was not to be ignored. There was undoubtedly *something* on the balcony outside the window.

Reluctantly I clambered out of bed, wondering vaguely what I could use as a weapon. As there appeared to be nothing immediately to hand, I very gingerly opened a crack in the wooden shutters and peered out. The moon shone brightly, illuminating the old stonework and silhouetting the tall trees against the horizon.

I had no difficulty in picking out our visitors. A pair of long-

eared owls sat on the balustrade, bowing and cooing to each other in loving courtship. I signalled urgently to Diana to come and have a look but in her haste she knocked something over on the dressing table and the two lovers spread their wings and launched themselves silently into the night.

One of the most exciting of our bird population round the house were the capercailzies. I had caught glimpses of these great birds during my winter walks through the pine woods. On one occasion I had come across a big cock roosting in a low larch tree. I was almost on top of him before he saw me and he took off like a rocket, blasting a way for himself through the surrounding branches so that for some time afterwards broken twigs continued to fall marking his line of departure.

The capercailzie is the most dramatic of all our resident game birds. The cock bird measures almost three feet from the tip of his ivory white beak to the tip of his tail and resembles nothing more than a dark coloured turkey. The hen bird is considerably smaller but makes up for it by her bright colouring with a broad cinnamon band across her chest.

The caper used to be much prized for its food value and so assiduously hunted that by the beginning of the last century they became extinct. The Marquis of Breadalbane reintroduced them on his Taymouth Castle Estate in 1837, since then they have increased mightily until once again they are not uncommon on Tayside and in particular on Rohallion Hill. I heard them more often than I saw them. The call of the caper is quite distinctive. It resembles the noise made by knocking two empty coconut shells together to reproduce the sound of a galloping horse. Starting slowly it gets faster and faster until the knocks run together in one continuous stream of noise. It is from this that it gets its name, capercailzie being roughly translated as "the horse of the woods".

One of their favourite habitats is on a wooded knoll behind the house in the old Buffalo Park, known as Duncan's Camp. Why this particular outcrop should have got this name nobody really knows although the romantics declare that it was where Duncan rested before his march against Macbeth ensconsed in Glamis Castle.

It is when the caper cocks are courting that they are to be seen at their most dramatic and it was something I was anxious to witness. Inconsiderately the performance only takes place at first light so it meant an early start with no guarantee that the loss of sleep would be rewarded.

When the alarm went off on the morning I had chosen for my expedition I rose reluctantly, wondering whether in fact it was worth getting up at such an unearthly hour. Of all the family I am the one who likes my sleep the most but I could get no one to accompany me on this venture – not even Charlie who is the keenest about birds. When I stepped outside the front door, however, all my reluctance vanished. There was no moon but the air was clean and sharp, making me catch my breath. There had been a white frost during the night and a myriad stars overhead sparkled with a wonderful brightness.

I climbed the steep hill above the house stopping every now and again to get my wind back for the cold made breathing difficult. As I got higher I could see away to the south the faint flush of the lights of Perth and, thinking of the sleeping world, I felt exalted, almost Godlike. That anyone should be laying in their beds on such a morning as this seemed suddenly extraordinary.

Of course in my anxiety not to be too late I had got up far too early. When I got to Duncan's Camp there was still no sign of dawn breaking and I settled down with my back against a large boulder to wait. It seemed a long time before the sky started to lighten over Rohallion Hill and the stars grew dimmer. Close at hand a deer barked and a skein of geese passed low overhead on their way from the Tay estuary to feed inland.

Suddenly it was quite light and the fir trees stood out clearly where a moment before they had only been a dark mass. I was just beginning to think that the main object of my expedition was to be fruitless when I heard behind me a sharp clear noise like the rasping of a file on metal. Peering over the top of my boulder and not more than ten yards distant I could make out two capercailzie cocks facing each other in a small clearing, their wings trailing on the ground and their tails spread out behind them. Then they started to dance.

In a short time they were joined by a third cock and then a fourth. They circled round each other like prize fighters in a boxing ring, sometimes strutting stiff legged, their hackles belligerently ruffled. At the same time they gave vent to a series of almost indescribable noises. The rasping noise would give way to a deep guttural gurgling in their throats alternating with a sort of wheezing whistle.

I was so absorbed in watching this ritual dancing that at first I did not notice the hen birds who had gathered round in a rough circle watching the performance with mesmeric intentness. Every now and again another bird would drop down out of a tree or appear from the surrounding bushes until there must have been over twenty of them either joined in the dancing or in the outer circle.

The whole performance must have lasted about half an hour before the numbers started to dwindle. Pairs began to slip off into the trees until finally there were again only two cock birds left fencing with each other and a handful of hens. In the end one of the cocks, sensing perhaps that the attention of the audience was beginning to wander, suddenly took off and went planing down the hillside on outstretched wings. I watched him whilst he glided over the treetops to the other side of the valley and when I looked back at the arena the others too had disappeared.

When I got back to the house Diana was already up. There were hot rolls on the table, bacon was sizzling on the stove and there was a smell of coffee in the air. I was filled with a great sense of wellbeing and contentment.

"You look extraordinarily cheerful," said Diana. "Why don't you get up before dawn every morning?"

For the life of me I could not think why not.

*   *   *

I have not yet introduced a most important member of the household – Sara, our King Charles spaniel.

Before we had decided to leave Buckinghamshire I had with great reluctance parted with my labrador, Mist. I know a lot of people keep labradors as household pets and perhaps if Mist had never led an active life as a gun dog she would have been more settled. As it was she fretted for more activity and became so much a one-man dog that she got quite neurotic if ever I went away. In the end I gave her to my brother Gordon who took her to his farm up in the hills where with plenty of work to do she settled down happily.

As a family we have always had a dog and feel that something is missing without one. With the departure of Mist, therefore, we started to look for a successor but argument raged furiously as to what we should have.

It was on one of our visits to Scotland that my mother told us about a local breeder who had a new litter of King Charles spaniels.

"Pooh," said I, "a lap dog."

"Don't they yap rather?" said Diana; but just the same we went along to have a look and that settled the matter.

Sara was the only unsold one of the litter.

"She's going to be far too big," the lady breeder told us. "No good for showing."

As one of my pet aversions is show dogs this was a good mark in my estimation but I still thought I might take advantage of it.

"You will be letting her go a bit cheaper than the rest then," I suggested.

It was a suggestion which was greeted with scorn. She could sell all her progeny three times over, the lady told us loftily. If we did not make up our minds on the spot it would be too late.

Hurriedly we closed the deal.

Three weeks later, when she was weaned, we drove Sara – Sarabande of Buckney to give her her full title – back to Kinloch, clutching her pedigree which proved that she came from a long line of champions. She seemed to be quite unconcerned at leaving the bosom of her family and stood up on her tiny hind legs on Diana's lap with her forepaws on the dashboard, survey-ing the big world with great interest. Then for good measure she spent a penny all over Diana's new skirt.

By the time we came to move into Rohallion, Sara was com-pletely established as the family favourite. To my delight she exhibited none of the characteristics which would have endeared her to the judges at Crufts. As we had been warned she grew far larger than is acceptable for her breed and her nose became positively patrician when compared with the Pekinese type noses of the champions. Above all she did not have the nervous yap of over-bred dogs. She tolerated us all with the greatest of good nature and, unlike Mist, shared her favours equally amongst the family.

As if to demonstrate her impartiality Sara established a night time routine for herself from which she would not be moved. When Jo-Jo, as the youngest, went early to bed she would accompany her upstairs and lie on her bed until she was asleep. Then she would come down of her own accord and wait until it was Charlie's turn when she would perform the same service for him. Finally she would settle down in her basket by the kitchen stove where she would remain until just before it was Diana's getting up time. Diana is an early riser but at whatever time she opened the bedroom door Sara would be sitting there waiting patiently for her to emerge. She would never scratch at the door to get in but the moment it was opened she would leap joyously onto our bed and burrow under the bedclothes where she would remain as quiet as a mouse until it was my time to get up and dress.

I suppose all dog owners are proud of their pet's intelligence and regard it as something out of the ordinary and in this we are no exception. During all the years I kept yellow labradors I have always trained them to the gun and expected them to be reasonably proficient and I have always been careful to buy dogs from a good working strain. For a time the activities of breeders who mated their yellow labradors for show rather than work almost completely destroyed the usefulness of the breed and it is only recently that the fault has started to be corrected. The encouragement of the right characteristics in dogs by selective breeding is of vital importance and I was slightly worried that the long line of show champions from which Sara was descended would make her less the sort of dog I wanted as a family pet. At risk of annoying a great number of people I will say that I have generally found dogs bred for show to be of lower intelligence than their less aristocratic brethren. One of the most lovable qualities of an out-and-out mongrel is its bright intellect. Perhaps they have to be that way to survive.

From her very earliest days Sara showed that she was remarkably bright and it was not long before she had mastered a considerable vocabulary. Dogs should not, any more than children, be addressed in baby language. To be exhorted to come 'walkies' and have 'din-dins' is absurd when a dog is quite capable of understanding normal speech.

If I went into the drawing room and found Sara sitting in my chair, which she always did if she thought she would get away with it, it was only necessary to say in a quiet voice "Go to your own chair" or more simply "beat it" for her to obey at once. If someone were to say casually "I think I will go for a walk" she would at once rush to the front door and wait in an agony of impatience and a mention of the fact that it was time to eat would send her scuttling through to the kitchen. We soon learned that if we did not want to raise her hopes we had to resort to spelling any word she was familiar with.

Above all she was anxious to prove on every possible occasion that she had a courage far greater than any mere toy dog. The rabbits, of course, which nibbled away cheerfully on our front lawn were child's play and not really worthy of her metal but if anyone arrived at the house with a larger dog she would bully it unmercifully until she had established her superiority and to come across cattle or horses when out for a walk roused her most ferocious instincts.

I only once saw her really got the better of. I was sitting in my study one morning trying to complete my daily quota of words when I was disturbed by the most pitiful cries outside the front door. I rushed out to find Sara cowering in abject terror against the door whilst an irate roe deer stood over her with head lowered and pawing the ground angrily. I recognised her as the mother of two fawns which she was rearing in a little copse scarcely thirty yards from the house. I had not even told the children about them so that she would be left in peace. Sara must have come on them in her morning blitz on the rabbits and aroused all the mother's protective instincts. I had to give the outraged mother a hard slap on the nose before she trotted off back to her babies, her head held proudly high.

Sara was very chastened for several days after that but she was luckier than she knew. By a thoughtful provision of Mother Nature the hooves of hinds develop an almost razor-like sharpness when they produce their fawns. This only lasts for a matter of a fortnight whilst the young are at their most vulnerable. Then they become blunt again but during this period their hooves are such formidable weapons as to be capable of cutting an enemy like a fox in half with a single blow. This one must have regarded Sara more as a tiresome nuisance who had to be taught a lesson than as a serious threat to her family.

Of course, in addition to Sara, it was inevitable that the children should start to collect pets of every sort. There were exotic rabbits which inevitably escaped to cross breed with wild mates and produce young of wonderful colours, there were tadpoles if they can be classed as pets, dredged from the loch and which never quite seemed to live long enough to turn into frogs and there were cats of every description.

The trouble with our cats was that we usually got them from some neighbouring farmer to save them from a watery grave and farmyard kittens never really get tame the way domestically reared ones do. They would get into the habit of wandering off into the woods and reappearing days later. Sometimes they did not reappear at all. One large tortoiseshell went off with a genuine wild cat of which we have quite a few and had her kittens under the outdoor larder. They were tawny eyed with rings right round their tails and as wild as could be. As I considered it an un-neighbourly act to increase the number of predators preying on Jimmy Wemyss' young pheasants I was about to call him in to have them destroyed when peering under the larder one morning, I found that the mother must have divined my intentions and carried them off into the undergrowth. Another mark against the cats was that they were apt to attack our fantail pigeons which were so tame that they waddled around under our feet on the lawn and were easy game.

In the end a decision was made to get rid of all cats which immediately resulted in a dramatic increase in the mouse population. It was at this stage that Mary stepped into the breach and appointed herself Chief Executioner of Mice. It became a familiar sight to come into the kitchen to see her elegant posterior protruding from the cupboard under the kitchen sink while she was setting her traps. In the height of the mouse season it was not unusual to get a bag of four or five brace each morning until Mary's efforts got on top of the problem.

Derek was responsible for another addition to the household which proved to be something of a Greek gift. One day we were partaking of a little refreshment in the Branch Office when he announced that he had the answer to a problem we were having in keeping the thistles down around the back quarters of the house.

Goats he told us, just loved thistles.

"You get a couple of goats," he said, "and your problems are over."

"Where would we get them and how much would they cost?" I asked.

"Weeeell now, come to think of it," he said, his eyes opening innocently wide in an expression I was later to come to know and distrust. "It so happens that I have a couple of goats outside at the moment which I could let you have as a great favour."

Of course I should have cross-examined him carefully as to where the goats had come from and why he was giving them away, but such is the trustfulness of my nature that I accepted his offer with alacrity and even thanked him warmly for his generosity. After all, was not Derek known in the village as Honest John?

I picked up Adam and Eve that afternoon and from the moment of letting them loose we had problems.

That is not to say that they were not the most endearing of creatures. The children loved them and spent much of their time having long wrestling matches with them. Adam in particular enjoyed having pushing contests with them, spreading his forelegs wide apart and lowering his head to butt against them with all his might. Jo-Jo and Charlie would push in the opposite direction until they all fell over in a heap. Then he would stand over them, his lips curled back in a triumphant smile while he waited for them to gather themselves together again for a further trial of strength.

As to eating the thistles, however, they proved to be a dead loss. At the same time they would eat everything else in sight. Soon our herbaceous border which Diana had cultivated with great pride resembled nothing more than a stricken battlefield. One morning we awoke to find that they had pushed down the wire netting which protected the lettuce bed from the rabbits and devoured the lot. Nothing delighted them more than to discover some flower budding quietly in a corner and nip off its head.

It also became impossible to leave the back or the front door open. Not only did they love getting into the house but their special delight was to climb the stairs. If ever they went missing we would be almost sure to find them sleeping peacefully on somebody's bed.

When they found themselves shut out and bored with their own company they would stand on their hind legs and beat a tattoo with their hooves against the windowpanes until, fearful that they would break the glass, we would rush out and drive them away. Meantime the thistles and weeds flourished mightily.

In the end, tired of brushing up goat droppings on the carpets and in despair of ever having any sort of a garden, we decided that they would have to go. We asked all round the district for anyone who would give them a home but there were no takers. Finally we advertised them and only got one reply from some- one who wanted only a nanny. When they arrived I tried to persuade them to take both but to no avail.

"We are breeders and you see we only want a nanny," they explained. Reluctantly I agreed to let Eve go on her own. Whilst we were talking the telephone rang and I left them alone whilst I answered it. I got back to find them loaded up and ready to go.

Five minutes later they were back looking rather embarrassed. They had, they explained, loaded Adam instead of Eve. I could only hope that they would be more selective when it came to picking a mate for her.

It was some time later that we had a telephone call from Glasgow from someone who had urgent need of a billy and was prepared to send a van all the way to pick him up. To my horror when the van arrived punctually at three o'clock the following afternoon I learned that it came from the University of Glasgow Veterinarian Department. At once I had terrible visions of Adam coming under the vivisectionist's knife. With relief I learned that he too was required for breeding purposes and had a harem of wives waiting for him. His future at least seemed secure.

The goats had scarcely departed before I got unwittingly involved in another stock-keeping enterprise. It came about in the most unexpected way. Really the person who must bear the greatest responsibility was Edith Robertson, the energetic and charming wife of Bruce the cathedral minister.

Edith was an enthusiastic organiser of good works to raise money for the Church and each year ran a mammoth Bring and Buy affair in the village. Everyone round about was canvassed to make some contribution to the sale and was also expected to make a purchase. Normally Diana or I would have attended the sale but as it so happened neither of us were able to do so. Shortly before it took place I ran into one of our local lairds and found that he was in a similar situation.

"I'll tell you what," I said suddenly struck with inspiration, "I'll buy whatever you send if you will buy what I send." And so it was agreed.

So far as I can now recollect I sent some wine, thinking that at least it would be something my neighbour would appreciate. His sense of humour, however, got the better of him.

Next day I was called to the door by the arrival of a Land Rover.

"Where do you want your sheep putting?" the driver asked.

"What sheep? I haven't bought any sheep."

"Oh yes you have. They were sold to you at the Church sale."

So there I was, lumbered once again.

In fact I was not displeased. For some time I had been wondering what use I could make of a field I had down by the stables and the sheep provided an answer. Diana and I had visions of fattening them up for the Christmas market and selling them at a great profit and perhaps even keeping one to cut up for the deep freeze we intended to buy. An example of just reward for Christian virtue.

Again our hopes were to be dashed.

A couple of months later when the sheep were beginning to come along well, the Brooner arrived at the house whilst I was away in Perth.

"I hear you have some sheep you might sell," he told Diana.

Diana, like myself, has a soft spot for the Brooner and likes to pull his leg.

"You'll have to get up early to get our sheep," she said, "They are as wild as March hares. They'd have the legs even off someone as smart as yourself."

"Don't worry yourself," he said complacently. "I already have them in the back of my van. It's just a matter of what you want for them."

That nonplussed her completely and to add to her confusion she had no idea what they might be worth.

"You'll have to wait until Douglas gets back. I don't even know how much he paid for them."

"I thought you wore the trousers in this house," said the Brooner, playing on her vanity.

"Suggest a price," snapped Diana who is as good at striking a bargain as anyone when she knows what she is talking about.

The argument went on for a long time with Diana trying to push up the Brooner on his first suggestion.

Eventually she stuck on £9.50.

"O.K.," said the Brooner, "we'll toss £10 or £9." Diana lost. It was only after he had driven away triumphantly that she realised that we did not want to sell them anyway. Still it was a fair price and I noticed with satisfaction that that winter the price in the open market slumped.

10

The variety of bird and animal life around Rohallion was a never ending source of delight to us.

Each morning as I bumped my way down the drive to take the children to school there would be deer browsing on the sweet grass on the verges. They would wait until the car was almost level with them before moving. Then they would race alongside us for about a hundred yards before turning to either right or left and with a graceful leap clear the high stone dykes and disappear into the woods.

Often we would come across woodcock taking a dust bath in the middle of the roadway. They were often so absorbed in this pleasure that I had to get out of the car to shoo them away. At other times we would see them when we were out walking, crouched in the bracken so close that we could almost touch them no doubt believing that their protective colouring made them invisible. I have always heard since a boy that the woodcock is the only bird which carries its own young whilst in flight but for every person who claims this to be true there is another who will deny it.

Several pairs of woodcock habitually nest around the house and one afternoon as I was taking a short cut through a wood down to the stables I was able finally to confirm the truth about the matter. I saw two woodcock chicks run up the track in front of me before darting into the bracken. When I reached the spot where they had disappeared I stopped and parted the fronds with my stick to see what had happened to them. Suddenly with a great fluttering the mother bird rose from the cover and I could see quite clearly one of the chicks held firmly between her powerful thighs. She made heavy weather of getting off the ground but once clear of the bracken rose easily above the young fir trees.

Almost the commonest birds as well as the most colourful are the pheasants. Some days one could count almost fifty by the side of the avenue, the cocks strutting and preening themselves in front of the hens or engaging in mock fights with their rival males. During the breeding season everybody in the house is under strict orders to keep to the woodland paths when out walking and to have their dogs under control for they are temperamental mothers who will desert their eggs at the slightest disturbance unlike the partridge who when sitting close will sometimes allow herself to be picked up and replaced on her nest.

The variety of the smaller birds is legion. Ferocious robins jealously guarding their territory, timid Jenny Wrens, Goldfinches, Woodpeckers, Treecreepers, Wagtails and Jays. House Martins and Swallows nest under the eaves of the house and swoop gracefully over the loch to pick the flies off the surface of the water and high in the sky hawks are sometimes to be seen, hovering motionless, ready to pounce on their prey.

For two years running there was a pair of peregrine falcons, surely the most graceful and certainly the rarest of our indigenous hawks, which I hoped were going to nest on a high outcrop of rock which could be easily seen from the house but, alas, each year they thought better of it.

Particularly in the winter almost every species of duck visits the loch and we constantly have the field glasses out identifying each new arrival. On occasions even Canada Geese pay us a passing visit whilst a pair of herons infuriate me by fishing for trout right under my indignant nose.

Bottom of my popularity list amongst our birds are the predatory starlings. They are messy, noisy and greedy. In the cold winter months when the colourful tits are feeding on the bird tray they will descend like school bullies and drive them all away whilst they gorge to their heart's content.

There is only one pair of starlings for whom I have a modicum of affection. They nest each year in a gap in the woodwork above the porch. When their young hatch the parents' efforts to keep pace with the gross appetites of their young are quite prodigious. Even in the driest weather they keep up a constant shuttle service returning to the nest every few seconds with their beaks full of worms. As our children are continually in a state of despair to find even a few worms for their fishing expeditions, where the starlings get them from is a mystery.

If the grounds round Rohallion are a naturalist's paradise so, too, are they a paradise for children. Although Diana struggles manfully to maintain a few flower beds and patches of vegetables, the rabbits, the pigeons and the deer see that these are kept to the bare minimum. Nor are the lawns of such perfection that they cannot be used for cricket, or badminton, football or croquet or simply as somewhere were they can ride roughshod on their bicycles.

From our earliest days at Rohallion we became used to the children disappearing for hours on end, turning up for meals grubby and exhausted. The rhododendrons are clumped in dense masses completely surrounding the loch, climbing the hill behind and, beyond the lawns forming a solid block of perhaps four acres through which run secret paths and hidden byeways. Some of the rhododendrons are immensely tall, rising to about thirty feet, a challenge to any ambitious young climber. When in June they flower in all their glory they and the massive azalea bushes provide a blaze of colour which I have seen matched nowhere else but to our growing family their greatest charm was as a playground of infinite variety.

The focal point of all these childrens' games was 'the big tree' – the giant Douglas fir at the end of the loch which is so massive that all four of them with their arms outstretched could not circle its circumference.

The record books have it that the tallest Douglas fir in Britain is at a nearby beauty spot known as The Hermitage. It is 180 feet tall. I have not put it to the test but I would like to take a wager that our one is taller.

I think it was Neil, the most practically minded of our family, who was the main architect of the underground house which they constructed under the spread of the big tree. It started with the excavation of a single subterranean chamber and from that it grew and grew. Long passages led to other rooms branching off a single great hall which served as a communal living room and kitchen. A fireplace was built where meals were cooked over a wood fire and eaten reclining on earthen seats.

Fearful that one day the whole complex would collapse on top of them we insisted that as many escape hatches were installed as possible. This had an unnerving effect on visitors. We would take them down to look at the tree when suddenly a head would pop up out of the ground yards away, then another and another. Visitors' children, too, suffered dreadfully. After a session in the underground house they would emerge with smoke-blackened faces and their best clothes caked with a particularly clinging mixture of clay and earth. On subsequent visits the parents would be wiser and dress them in their oldest rags.

There is a small island on the loch and this became Charlie's particular refuge. A few scrubby Spruce trees grow on it but under the bushes the duck and the waterhens come to nest and to lie on one's stomach looking down into the clear water is to see fat trout feeding lazily. Whenever Charlie has a special friend to stay he takes him out to 'his' island where they have most of their meals. It is the highest honour he can bestow.

My own favourite time in the summer is the long evenings when one can sit outside and watch the dusk creep across the hillside. High in the sky the crows and pigeons are winging their way home to their roosting places and above one's head the bats perform their aerial ballet, twisting and diving as they feed.

Diana professes to be terrified of bats, subscribing to some strange superstition that they have a predilection for ladies' hair and that once they have taken hold they will not let go. On one occasion a tiny pipistrelle fluttered into our bedroom as she was getting dressed to go out for the evening. She fled from the room and would not return until I had with great difficulty managed to capture the intruder in a landing net with the result that we were late for dinner.

Once when Peter the Provost had been replacing some slates on the roof he must have disturbed a bats' nest for I later picked up two baby long-eared bats on the stairs. As they seemed to be unhurt I wanted to try and rear them.

Peter was horrified.

"Bats!" he exclaimed. "I'd kill every bat I could get the head of my hammer to."

"What have you got against bats?" I protested.

"The stink! There's nothing stinks like bats. You get rid of those bats or you'll regret it."

Alas, they proved impossible to rear so I don't know whether I would have regretted it or not.

Other companions in those long hours of dusk are the badgers. Seated quietly on the terrace I used to watch for them as they crept cautiously out onto the lawn, sniffing suspiciously. In the half light the white patches of their coats made them look almost ghostly.

A pair of badgers made their home down a big hole they dug in the chicken run with an exit outside the wire. From this point of vantage they were able to live almost exclusively on hens eggs but I did not mind. I was compensated by being able to watch them bring up their young which used to come out and play boisterous games as darkness fell.

In midsummer it never quite gets completely dark but it seems all too short a time before the nights start closing in again.

Winter brings its own pleasures and problems. The main problem is how to keep the house warm.

Both the morning room and the large drawing room have enormous fireplaces which take logs three or four feet long and the task of carrying these small tree trunks in from the wood-shed usually devolves on me. I was rash enough on one occasion to give it as my opinion that it takes a man to build a decent fire and I have never been allowed to forget it. Apart from the labour involved the trouble is that people will interfere with my fires once they are built. Diana is the worst offender.

"Huh! Pretty poor fire you've got there," she will say and, crossing the room, give one of the logs a derisive kick whereupon the whole skilfully constructed edifice collapses and has to be patiently reconstructed.

Fires, however, are by no means the end of our heating troubles. The long corridors which run the whole length of the house are frigid tunnels of air in spite of having space heaters at regular intervals all of which never seem to be working at the same time. Most of the rooms are also fitted with under-carpet heating which we used freely when we first moved in – until we got out first electricty bill. After that, in an effort to save elec-tricity we equipped ourselves with endless paraffin heaters which we scattered around the house. Paraffin heaters, however, require constant attention. To overlook their demands is to have them burn dry which apart from creating a dreadful smell usually entails buying a new wick.

Anticipating one of the recurrent national fuel emergencies I had the foresight to install a five hundred gallon storage tank for paraffin and had it filled just before the oil companies introduced rationing. It was Charlie's job to fill a five gallon drum from this each day before going to school. All went well for a week. Then one day he put the drum in place and turned on the tap and wandering away forgot to turn it off again whereupon five hundred gallons overflowed into the ground and we had to go back to buying it at a few gallons at a time.

Now we have mobile gas heaters which we wheel from room to room but all we can hope to achieve is to have oases of warmth and put on our overcoats when we go upstairs to bed. We try to convince ourselves and the children that to sleep in a cold bedroom is healthy and refuse to allow them to smuggle up heaters. I remember one particularly cold night when Fiona appealed for a relaxation of the rule.

"Nonsense," snorted Diana. "Run along upstairs – and remember to turn on my electric blanket as you go past!"

One result of this Spartan regime is that none of us ever has a cold.

On the whole the trials of winter – icy roads, cars which won't start and the rest – are more than compensated for by the pleasures.

As a family we are all great players of indoor games. From an early age the children have learned the intricacies of Chess, Backgammon and Bridge as well as a limitless number of other card games from Poker to Snap. There is usually a large jig-saw puzzle in the corner of the morning room which sometimes takes weeks to complete and old favourites like Monopoly are continually being given an airing. Television is banished to a room at the back of the house and although everyone has their own favourite programmes television viewing is not generally considered half as entertaining as sitting round a roaring fire squabbling over the rules of one game or another. We are by no means a highbrow family – just a very competitive one.

Another of the pleasures of the long dark nights is that more attention is devoted to gastronomy. During the summer our eating habits are casual. The family or our guests wander in and out of the kitchen helping themselves to anything that is easy like cornflakes or baked beans or salads. There are really no set meal times. In winter it is different. For one thing there is a ready supply of game and it seems a pity to roast say a brace of pheasants without involving oneself in all the bits and pieces which go with them like fried breadcrumbs and cranberry sauce.

My father used to say that there was only one way to eat capercailzie. First, he claimed, you should bury it in the ground for up to three weeks. Then dig it up, pluck it and stuff it with a very large onion studded with cloves. Place in the oven and cook for a long time basting it the while with its own fat. When considered thoroughly done remove the bird from the oven, take out the onion and throw the bird away. Eat the onion. Enough for one.

Of course father was wrong. The caper is a delicious bird to eat and many a feast we have had off one. It is a peculiar bird in that the flesh is dark when you first start to carve it but the nearer you get to the breastbone the lighter it becomes so that it is finally as white as chicken.

By trial and error Diana has developed many original recipes like venison cooked with an oxtail which brings out the flavour and keeps it moist or pheasant done in gin though quite how she discovered that this much improves the bird history does not relate.

In the old days there used to be a curling match played every winter on Robin's Dam. I am quite sure that winters must have been harder in the last century for there are few big houses round about which do not have their own artificially made curling ponds and there was great rivalry between teams made up of the rival estate workers. Now they have either fallen into disrepair or serve a purpose as duck ponds. The hard weather is not nearly consistent enough to rely on for regular matches.

I have often been told that on one occasion when there was a two day curling match – or bonspiel as it is properly called – on Robin's Dam the curlers left their stones overnight on the ice for they are heavy objects to carry home. Alas there came a sudden thaw and next morning they arrived to find that the ice had given way and all their stones had sunk into the mud on the bottom. Legend has it that they were for the most part Ailsa Craig stones – the aristocrat of curling stones and hard to come by these days so I have a small fortune sunk in my loch. Maybe one day if I have a guest who is a skin diver I will set him to work.

11

ONE OF the excitements of late summer is the Highland Games which are held by the side of the River Braan between Birnam and Inver. It would be hard to imagine a more lovely setting with the pine-clad hills surrounding the arena on all sides. With scarcely a house in sight it must look much as it did when the games were first held there a hundred and fifty years ago.

'Our' Games are scarcely amongst the best known in Scotland. The Braemar Games, with their Royal Patronage, receive world wide publicity every year and even Games much closer at hand, like Crieff and Pitlochry and Lochearnhead, are on a much grander scale. Birnam Games, however, have much to commend them and are well thought of by the stars who travel all over the country in search of prize money. Runners and cyclists, pipers, dancers and tug o' war teams as well as the 'heavies' who toss the caber, throw the hammer and put the weight converge on Birnam to compete against each other and take on any local athletes who fancy their chances.

The day of the Games also marks the visit of the travelling Fair who occupy the bottom end of the field. There are dodgem cars and roundabouts, shooting galleries and coconut shies, candy floss and toffee apples. All in all the Games are something everybody looks forward to, young and old alike.

On the day of the games there is a general air of festivity in Dunkeld and Birnam. The children have been up early and down at the field watching the tents being erected and the Fair folk making ready for the day's business. Hand written posters appear at the roadside to attract the passing-through trade who might otherwise be unaware of the important event, and there are extra police drafted in to control the expected crowd.

That first year there was great activity also at Rohallion. As

usual we had people staying so that our party numbered twelve. Soon after breakfast the preparations for the picnic began. Baps, which are the Scottish equivalent of breakfast rolls only much more delicious, had been bought in great quantities fresh from the baker and now had to be cut open to be spread with butter and filled with a great variety of cold meats, hard boiled eggs and lettuce. There were Thermos flasks to be filled with home-made soup, cold chicken to be cut into portions and wrapped in grease-proof paper, other flasks for tea and coffee and the corners of the picnic hampers to be filled up with apples, bananas and slices of fruit cake.

Derek at the Branch Office had warned me that the beer tent became impossibly crowded so I insured against any inconvenience with a good supply of adult refreshment. As Diana remarked rather acidly I always over-react to any danger of a shortage in that respect.

In spite of our determination to get to the ground early in order to secure a good place, it was already comfortably full by the time we arrived and cars were pouring in through the narrow gate nose to tail. We were lucky to get one car against the ringside and soon they were parked three deep behind us.

If the Birnam Games have a particular claim to eminence it is in the quality of the pipers who came from far and near to be judged each year. All round the outer perimeter of the ground there were pipers in full Highland dress, practising to themselves in any secluded corner they could find, right up until the moment when they would have to step before the judges.

The judges themselves, kilted and bonneted, sat in solemn conclave at the edge of the judging area, up and down which each competitor paced in turn with the traditional slow, controlled step. In the centre of the three adjudicators sat Archie Alves who is our Mary's uncle and himself a piper of great renown.

I was more used to seeing him in his smart railwayman's uniform, seeing one off on the London train at Birnam Station. A cheerful, happy man with a ready smile but today he looked solemn and even stern as he listened attentively to each piper. It would certainly be unbecoming to show any levity when an aside from him to his two fellow judges could dash the chances of young hopeful or mature performer alike.

By the time we had all settled ourselves on rugs spread in front of the car there was already considerable activity in the ring. The sprinters were hammering their starting blocks into place and the longer distance runners jogging round in their track suits whilst cyclists, bent over their low-slung handlebars, their bottoms high in the air, wobbled uncertainly over the uneven ground. To one side of the ring the Junior Highland Dancing competition had started. Four at a time they went through their paces, some of them tall and willowy, some of them scarcely two jam pots high, but all turned out beautifully, silver buttons and buckles gleaming and kilts of every imaginable tartan.

Soon others arrived to join our party. Mary appeared breathless, her dog trying to pull on its lead in one direction and her youngest child Joyce tugging in another whilst, at the same time she was burdened with baskets, rugs and other paraphernalia. Then came Eddie and Liz Butterworth with their young family looking for somewhere to sit. Eddie, a dyed-in-the-wool Midlander was in the process of building a timber and glass house on a loch he had recently acquired and now appeared thinly disguised as a Scotsman in a Highland bonnet and supporting himself with a long shepherd's crook.

The Chieftain of the Games, Donald Steuart-Fotheringham, arrived with his party to take their places in the open-sided tent reserved for him. The blaring music from the roundabouts competed stridently with the pipers and the Master of Ceremonies blew noisily into his microphone to make sure it was working. All around the ring the crowd buzzed with excited anticipation.

The competitive spirit at Highland Games is much in evidence and the crowd strongly partisan. Everyone is cheering on the local heroes, hoping they will do well against the semi-professionals. One of the great favourites with the crowd is an elderly grey haired sprinter whom rumour has it is nearing his sixtieth year and who has been coming to Birnam for so long as to be almost accepted as a local. The open hundred yards is a handicap event and when I saw him take his place on the starting blocks I did not think, considering his years, that he had been over-generously treated. However, he managed to hold on to beat the back marker, a young giant of eighteen summers, by a matter of inches while the crowd roared its approval.

Event followed event with an admirable lack of ceremony. The cyclists who had had the misfortune to be involved in spectacular tumbles at the sharp bends had scarcely time to clear the track before the crack of the Starter's pistol announced that the milers were on their way. The dancers danced on endlessly and the pipers paced solemnly to and fro before the judges whilst the 'heavies' took over the centre of the arena, flexing their muscles with practice throws.

The heavy events are perhaps the most eagerly looked forward to. There is the long-hafted hammer, the shot putting and the vertical throwing of the 14-pound weight over a bar, as well as the spectacular tossing of the caber. Currently the scene is dominated by two giants in the persons of Bill Anderson from Aberdeen and his great rival Arthur Rowe who is not a Scotsman at all but hails from Yorkshire. Whenever either of these mighty men are about to throw a hush falls all round the ground as the crowd wait with bated breath to see if yet another record is to be broken. There are however always up-and-coming men who press hard on the heels of the established stars. This year for example there was a young lecturer from Strathclyde University who, it was said, was well on his way to becoming a new champion and everybody was looking forward to seeing him perform.

In spite of the colourful events in the ring, the children found the attractions of the fairground even more fascinating. Fearful lest the younger ones would fall off the merry-go-round or suffer some similar disaster the grown-ups took turns at first to supervise them but as they all disappeared in different directions at once this soon proved impractical and we let them go their own ways. From time to time they would reappear triumphantly bearing coconuts, candy floss or other trophies and trying to wheedle some more money out of their parents. We made valiant efforts to resist their repeated demands but there always seemed to be somebody who would take pity on them and slip them a surreptitious couple of shillings. I know few children who are not shameless beggars and ours are certainly no exception.

In the midst of all this activity the social side of the gathering flourished mightily. Everyone from the village was there and it seemed that most of them turned up at some time or another where we were sitting, to have a word. Having commented favourably on the fineness of the weather and the size of the turn out and generally observed the formalities the question of a little refreshment would arise. It is not done to show undue eagerness at the offer of a drink. The usual reply is a guarded "I don't mind" which may fairly be translated as "What are we waiting for?"

Contrary to the Scotsman's reputation for being mean, which is a myth we rather like to encourage, it is almost impossible to offer him a drink and resist his insistence on giving you one back. On social occasions such as the Games or at local dances, many of them carry their own supply with them in the shape of a half bottle in the back pocket. For those not equipped in this way nothing would satisfy them but that I should accompany them to the refreshment tent where they could 'staun their haund'. This operation would inevitably result in getting involved with several other convivial souls whose only anxiety appeared to be that one's plastic cup should never be empty. When one finally escaped to hurry back to the car it was to find a new group of acquaintances discussing the weather and the size of the crowd and the whole process threatening to start all over again.

A welcome interruption came with the appearance of the pipe band of the Black Watch who now paraded up and down the arena playing brave music, the drum major stepping out in front throwing his heavy, silver-hilted stick high in the air whilst the cameras clicked, toes were set a-tapping and you could sense the whole crowd swelling with pride. There is surely no more inspiring music in the world than the skirl of the pipes and the beat of drums. I have heard pipe bands all over the world from the sands of the Libyan desert to the middle of Fifth Avenue, New York and they seldom fail to move me. I say seldom because I used to know the hereditary chieftain of an ancient Scottish clan whose family had lost their estates many generations ago. He still insisted, however, on being piped into dinner every night by the family piper. Even I, fond though I am of the pipes, found it a bit of a strain in a small suburban house in Ruislip! To hear the pipes at their best is to hear them surrounded by the lonely hills of the homeland.

As the afternoon wore on our party grew and grew. Two young Australian girls whose old van, gaily decorated with stickers and slogans was parked behind us, became somehow 'adopted'. They were merry as crickets and bubbling over with enthusiasm for all things Scottish. There was also Donald Mackenzie, a bronzed giant of a man who was home on leave from tea planting in India. Donald was an old friend but I viewed his arrival with some misgiving for where I was trying to stem the flow of drinks, mindful that someone would have to take the responsibility for driving home, Donald had quite contrary ideas. Every now and again he would disappear to return moments later with fresh supplies of beer and whisky which he insisted on offering to all and sundry with open handed generosity. What I had planned as an afternoon of quiet enjoyment in the warm sunlight threatened to develop into a baccanalia. To add to my embarrassment I noticed that the parties on either side of us were quietly sipping cups of tea and looking at us with obvious disapproval.

Fortunately events in the ring were now reaching a climax. Roars of applause greeted the efforts of the heavyweights with appropriate ooh's and aah's when throws went winging dangerously out of line. Suddenly a particularly loud burst of cheering resounded round the ring as a new competitor stepped into the base circle and prepared to throw. Traditionally the heavyweight men are dressed in kilts with big loose knitted sweaters which they discard when it comes their turn to throw. The newcomer took no heed of the tradition. He was wearing what looked like his best Sunday suit with his trousers tucked into his socks. As he stepped forward to take his turn he stripped off his jacket, loosened his tie and rolled up the sleeves of his white shirt. Then he spat on his hands and, picking up the weight, gave it a preliminary whirl round his head.

"And now," said the announcer, "let's have a little hush for the next competitor. Our local champion Ian Brown!"

"Good Heavens!" exclaimed Diana. "It's the Brooner."

And so it was. We all watched in astonishment as he whirled, light as a feather on his feet, and sent the weight sailing high against the blue sky. There was a moment's silence while the judges pegged and measured the throw and then a great shout of delight and cries of "Weel done, the Brooner" when the distance was announced. He hadn't beaten Rowe or Anderson but he was close up behind them, a good third.

I was still lost in admiration at this unexpected performance when Philip, Mary's son, arrived wearing a football shirt and great heavily-studded boots. He was dancing on his toes and shaking his arms loosely at his sides for all the world like an Olympic champion limbering up for the hundred metres.

"What on earth do you think you're doing?" I asked in astonishment.

"I'm in for the tug-o-war," he said. "Give us a beer 'till I get in the mood."

"You're no needin' any beer," said Mary severely. "You'll need all your puff."

"We train on beer," said Philip cheerfully, tipping half a can down his throat at one gulp. Then he trotted off, burping happily to join his mates who made up the Birnam team.

To my surprise and great delight they won their first pull against what looked like a much heavier side and only just lost the second after a titanic struggle. On the decider, however, they collapsed in an untidy heap and I made up my mind that next year I would have to talk to him seriously about his training methods.

The sun was now hanging low over Rohallion Hill and the shadows lengthening across the arena. The dancers still danced on but the last of the pipers had done his piece and the judges were in earnest conference totting up the score sheets. The announcer was tirelessly trying to drum up some interest in a sack race, the noise from the fair was more strident than ever and the canvas walls of the beer tent bulged dangerously as more and more thirsty customers pushed and strained to get near the bar.

It was time to leave and search parties were sent out to round up the children. They were eventually assembled clutching a wide variety of strange objects which they had gleaned in their perambulations around the side-shows. Improbably Jo-Jo had acquired a couple of very small goldfish in a water-filled plastic bag which she hugged tightly to her chest making their chance of survival until we could get them to Rohallion even more problematical.

Wisely Diana and I had left our own car near the exit so, muttering vaguely that we might see everyone later, we made a quick getaway to set the house in order in case anyone descended on us. In fact when we arrived back the evening was so warm and peaceful that we dropped exhausted into chairs on the terrace and sat watching the sun set in a bath of brilliant gold. The wood pigeons were winging their way in a long procession to roost in the dark pinewoods up the valley and the trout were rising busily, dotting the smooth surface of the loch with concentric rings.

We were just beginning to hope that no one had taken us at our word and, with our house guests going out to dinner, we would have a quiet evening recovering from the day's excitements when the roar of a high-powered engine announced the arrival of a most improbable procession. First came Eddie Butterworth in one of those long low motor cars which are all engine and only enough room inside to seat himself and one passenger. Following behind were his wife and sister-in-law with their joint children and behind them the Australian girls with sundry characters from the village piled in the back of their battered van and, behind them again our neighbours Peter and Ann Stock with their three young. Bringing up the rear, riding shot gun as it were, was the formidable figure of Donald Mackenzie, his hired limousine stacked high with crates of drink of every description.

The evening which followed was a memorable one. We sat outside in the long Scottish twilight. I was content to let Donald worry about bottles and glasses, a responsibility which he undertook with great enthusiasm. Diana and Ann fussed half-heartedly with plates of food in which nobody showed any great interest and conversation rolled on like a tide.

On occasions like this visiting children are well trained. The younger ones were popped into sleeping bags, later to be transferred unconscious to the back of cars and driven home to their own beds, whilst the older ones disappeared into the night and could be heard calling to each other like Indians in a Wild West film about to launch a night attack on the Palefaces.

Then the singing started. Liz and her sister Jane Nelson-Peebles, who has a growing reputation as a West End actress, harmonised the old Scottish songs, their voices rising pure and clear in the night air, while the 'indians' gathered round in an outer circle to listen in silence. The irrepressible Eddie who, before he had somehow drifted into becoming a property tycoon had qualified as a doctor at Edinburgh University, changed the

113

mood with some of the more disreputable songs from his student days, and not to be outdone the Australian girls launched into a selection of stirring ditties from Down Under. Even I, tone deaf though I may be, and in spite of Diana's protests, was allowed to give my rendering of "There's a wee Hoose 'mang the Heather" which is the only song of which I know all the words and which, although I say it myself, I sing with great feeling. It was a measure of the indulgent mood of the party that I was not shouted down after the first verse.

Another glorious dawn was already breaking before anybody could bring themselves to make a move. Donald Mackenzie was the last to leave. Fearing that his dedication to his duty as self-appointed barman might have had a detrimental effect on his capacity as a driver we begged him to stay and have a few hours' sleep before breakfast but he scornfully brushed aside our well intentioned offer.

"In India," he declared indignantly, "I frequently drive a hundred and fifty miles to a party and get back to start work on my estate by six in the morning. The trouble with you lot is that you have no stamina."

We watched him bounce off down the pot-holed drive with some trepidation while I, feeling remarkably fresh and relaxed, decided to dispense with bed altogether on such a wonderful morning and sat down to try and string some words together on my typewriter.

Two hours later when I was beginning to feel that it would after all have been better to have got some sleep, a car drew up with a flourish outside the front door and I watched with some dismay as the six foot four inches of the bold Mackenzie uncurled from behind the steering wheel. My dismay turned to alarm when I saw that he had discarded his jacket, his sleeves were rolled up and his bare arms were smeared with what looked very much like blood.

My worst fears were, however, not realised. It appeared that somewhere on his way home – history does not relate the exact spot of the awful deed – he had rounded a sharp bend and run slap into a roe deer, killing it instantly. Possibly for some reason connected with his long years in India, he had a large knife in the back seat. With this he had spent a happy hour skinning the beast and cutting it into joints.

114

"In India," he declared, "fresh meat putrefies by midday so I thought I would just bring you along a shoulder straight away. Now if you could tell me exactly where the Butterworths live . . ."

"Donald," I said, "if you think you're going to drive round the countryside delivering haunches of venison at this unearthly hour on a Sunday morning, you'd better think again. Go and have a bath and I'll get you some coffee."

This time he did as he was told. When I went up later with his coffee, it was to discover that he had found a spare bedroom and was sleeping like a babe.

Altogether it had been an eventful twenty-four hours in our placid life.

12

I will not pretend that by transporting my family from Buckinghamshire to the middle of Scotland I did away with all the small irritations of life at a stroke. The mere act of crossing the Border did not magically transform all my family into models of virtue or teach them to have more respect and consideration for me as the benign all-wise head of the household. Jo-Jo did not become any less noisy, Charlie was still apt to go into declines when he was thwarted and Neil and Fiona continued to quarrel with each other furiously over trivialities.

Even the calm of our new surroundings did nothing to cure Diana of her habit of bullying me first thing in the morning. The time to reproach a man for such small oversights as not paying the electricity bill or failing to get onto the plumber about a dripping tap is when he has breakfasted well and is enjoying the first pipe of the day, not when he is in the delicious limbo of half wakefulness, still trying to recapture the web of a fading dream.

On the whole, however, our everyday problems seemed much less pressing than they did in the South and the tempo of life was much more leisured. London which had once been the centre of all things for me seemed very far away indeed.

It was because of this mild euphoria that I found myself becoming increasingly irritated by the traffic which poured unceasingly up and down the A.9 and spilled over into all the quiet byways. In the South one grumbles about the traffic but one takes it in one's stride. Four hundred and fifty miles to the north I found myself regarding it with less tolerance.

My main complaint was not with the great lorries carrying the sinews of industry nor indeed so much with the number of cars, but in the way that they were driven. The A.9 is one of the most dangerous roads in the country but it would not be nearly

116

so perilous if motorway-conditioned drivers did not treat it as a multi-lane carriageway. These drivers are an easily recognised breed. If they cannot pass immediately they drive within a foot of one's back bumper, flashing their lights and generally behaving like spoilt children. When they do pass, cutting in again sharply to avoid oncoming traffic, and if one is uncivil enough to protest with a blast on the horn, they stick their arms out of their windows and stab the air with a two finger gesture which is far from Churchillian. No doubt they are largely downtrodden travellers selling something unexciting like toothpaste and enjoying their moments of living dangerously, but they have the power of putting up my bloodpressure to a dangerous level. In the summer when the holiday traffic is at its peak hardly a week passes but an unrecognisable wreck is towed into John Young's garage at the bottom of Birnam Hill. Tragically more often than not these grim reminders of the perils of the road are the victims rather than the aggressors.

On one occasion I was standing talking to John and looking at the latest wreckage to come in when a car drew up on the forecourt and the furious figure of a middle-aged man strode across to us.

"Where are my tools?" he shouted, shaking his fist under John's nose in his rage.

John is one of the mildest of men and was not unnaturally somewhat taken aback. When the man grew slightly more coherent it was revealed that he was the father of the driver of the wrecked car. His son was subsequently proved to have been completely responsible for the accident which had killed his girl friend although he himself had had a miraculous escape. The father's only concern was that it was *his* tools which had been in the back of the car. Now some of them were missing and he was threatening to sue John for their value! I'm glad to say that John's reaction was far from mild.

Perhaps the road-users who incurred my greatest displeasure were the caravanners. At weekends they would appear driving nose to tail, sometimes as many as half a dozen in procession, defying anyone to pass them. The lay-by just up from my driveway was always full of them, sitting in groups on their plastic chairs, their transistors blaring and scattering their debris around them.

Of course my attitude was wholly unreasonable. Not everyone can afford to take their families away for holidays in expensive hotels and what better way of enjoying the countryside which is everybody's birthright than by towing your holiday house behind you? Yet my dislike for them persisted. At least it did until I had a rather chastening experience.

I was driving back from Kinloch along the back road to Dunkeld and in a hurry to get to the butcher's before it shut when I caught up with a caravan progressing at a stately twenty-five miles an hour. The road was narrow and winding and I could see no prospect of getting past in the next ten miles.

"Just look at that," I exploded to Diana. "Damned fellow seems to think he owns the road. I tell you the sooner they tax caravans out of existence the sooner we will cure our traffic problems. Why can't he get a move on."

"You're not being very logical," Diana observed mildly. "Only yesterday you were calling down damnation on one of them who passed you at sixty miles an hour."

"Humpf!" I said and relapsed into an impatient silence.

Almost immediately afterwards the caravan slowed to a halt right on a bend in the road. Seizing my opportunity I squeezed past, changing up furiously but not before I had rolled down Diana's window and, leaning across her, delivered myself of a few choice epithets.

"Did you ever see anything like that in your life," I barked, "Of all the bloody fool places to stop!"

"If you would only use your eyes you would have realised that the nice man was stopping to let you past where he could see that the road was clear."

I was immediately overcome with the most dreadful remorse. Here was a really decent driver doing the right thing and I had to go and bawl at him.

Anyway we made Bert Wood's butcher's shop in time and later repaired to the Branch Office where, still full of contrition, I confessed to Derek what an ass I had made of myself.

I had just finished relating the incident when a stranger standing behind me said, "I'm glad you've cleared up the misunderstanding. You see it was my caravan."

He was a delightful man. He took me over to introduce me to his wife and kids and we exchanged drinks. I was so overcome that I offered him my ground to park his caravan on for as long as he liked to stay but he had booked in on a site further up the glen. We parted the best of friends and I have been noticeably less belligerent about caravanners ever since.

Shortly after this I was faced with another caravan problem of a rather different sort.

We were enjoying a peaceful afternoon sitting in the garden when we heard the noise of a car approaching down the drive. From long experience Diana and I have developed an old and crafty defence against unexpected visitors. I melt away while Diana quickly puts on a coat and goes to the front door. If it is someone we don't want to see she says brightly "Oh, what a terrible shame. We are just about to go out." If, on the other hand it is a welcome visit she says equally brightly "What a stroke of luck. We have just got in!"

This time however there was no time to employ such tactics. Our drinks were on the garden table and we were all too obviously very much at home. Our dismay increased when there appeared a large car drawing an equally impressive caravan. A moment later our old friend 'Rumpty' Lowther-Pinkerton was bounding across the gravel.

Although I have known Rumpty for many years I have never learned his proper first name or heard him called by anything but his nickname and the origins of that are obscure.

To realise how ludicrous was his sudden arrival towing a caravan I will have to introduce him. Rumpty is a large man who looks something like a cross between a Bishop and a Brigadier but beneath this formidable exterior there is a boyish enthusiasm which makes him instantly likeable. When I first met him he was working for the Special Branch of Scotland Yard and when we were changing for a game of squash one day I noticed that he carried a pistol in a holster strapped under his left armpit which impressed me greatly. Since then he had, I believe, become 'something in the City' and dresses the part in immaculately tailored suits and the correct hat for every occasion. He lives in some style with his wife, Sue, and a growing family in Suffolk and from time to time I see his name in the social columns of *The Times* as a guest attending some important function. I like to think that when the Prime Minister has some important decision to make, Rumpty is at his shoulder.

When I got over my surprise at seeing him I asked, "What are you doing with that . . . that *thing* attached to your motor car?"

"Oh you mean the caravan," he said with an airy wave of his hand. "I just thought I would take Sue and the family for a touring holiday. Jolly comfortable you know."

It transpired that he had spent the past few days parked in the grounds of his kinsman, Lord Lonsdale's house in Cumberland.

"James told me you had a nice little place up here so I just thought we would drop by," he explained. He stayed for a few days but, although I questioned him narrowly I finally had to be satisfied that there was no more glamorous or sinister explanation for his visit.

The children insisted on taking over the caravan and Rumpty and Sue moved into the house while we had a happy time drinking too much whisky and catching up on the doings of old friends.

When he decided that the time had come for him to move on I was delighted to find him for once in his life slightly stumped. Scotland was off his beat and he did not know where to stay next.

"Trouble with these thingummies is that you can't just park them anywhere you know," he said with an air of ingenuous surprise. "Don't much fancy those caravan sites even if you can get into them. Don't trust the water."

In the end I suggested ringing an old friend who had a large estate near Inverness. Rumpty was delighted so I picked up the 'phone. The butler answered. No, His Lordship was away for the day. Would I care to ring in the evening?

"Don't worry," I said gaily. "A friend of mine is coming north and would like to park his caravan in the castle grounds. I take it that would be alright."

There was a long pause at the other end of the line. "A caravan did I hear you say, sir?" said the butler, and I could hear him breathing heavily. "I take it you are unaware that His Lordship is Chairman of the Anti-Caravanners Association."

I replaced the receiver gently and remembered thankfully that I had not given my name.

I got Rumpty eventually fixed up with a Duchess and he went off happily. Somehow I always seem to put my foot in it when I get mixed up with caravans.

If the warm weather brought in its train rashes of weekend motorists and epidemics of caravans there were many compensations. Not the least was that the loch which remained frozen over for most of the winter, warmed up early on in the summer so that the children were swimming in it regularly by the beginning of June. Instead of putting the long boat in the boat house I now moored it on the bank below the house so that they could dive off the end of it into about seven feet of crystal clear water. At first I used to insist that there would be no swimming unless there was a grown-up in the little fibreglass dinghy I had bought in the Spring, ready to swoop down on any child who got into difficulties. The bottom of the loch shelves sharply to about eighteen feet and Charlie in particular who was just learning to swim was apt to strike out ambitiously for the middle. Also at weekends children came in from round about so that whoever was supervising had to keep their eyes peeled with perhaps a dozen kids of all ages from the paddling to the expert stage splashing and ragging each other.

As summer wore on however and swimming became such a routine matter we relaxed our strict supervision and the little boat was only manned when some event like an across-the-loch and-back-swim was being organised. Moreover we had now increased our navy to include a raft and a rubber dinghy so a refuge was never very far away.

Only Jo-Jo remained a non swimmer. From time to time she would make valiant efforts, thrashing wildly with her arms and shouting "Look at me! Look at ME! I'm swimming!" But she always had one toe firmly on the bottom. For the most part however she preferred to sit at the far end of the long boat, her feet dangling in the deep water and splashing anyone who came near.

Although we had given up having someone responsible in a boat we still maintained a rule that there should always be someone on the bank keeping a general eye on the proceedings. It was a duty we mostly imposed on our guests, leaving us free to go about our general chores. On this particular day watch was being kept by Roddie who was one of Jo-Jo's godparents. Roddie is a young man of unnerving brilliance who presents a front of languid weariness to the world. He had just taken an honours degree in Chinese at Cambridge and was contemplating offering his services to the Foreign Office. We all love him dearly but I for one doubted his competence as an aquatic supervisor on the grounds that he was generally so deeply engrossed in some weighty tome and, one felt, not in close touch with what was going on.

Jo-Jo was at her usual post at the end of the boat when the inevitable happened. One moment she was splashing vigorously with her legs and the next moment she had over-balanced and plunged out of sight into the water. I have never regarded Roddie as an athletic person but he now moved like greased lightning. In an instant he was down the bank and plunging into the loch. Jo-Jo was dragged to the surface, spluttering and coughing, less frightened than furiously angry at the indignity she had suffered.

Poor Roddie. Far from earning Jo-Jo's eternal gratitude for saving her from a watery grave, she refused to speak to him for several days, obviously feeling that in some way he was responsible for the whole affair.

Jo-Jo's accident could have been serious but for the most part there is something hilariously funny about people falling into the water in the same classic tradition as slipping on a banana skin. One episode in particular sticks in my mind.

It happened one Spring that two old friends had come to stay at John's hotel for the goose shooting and, finding that most of the birds had already departed to their breeding grounds in the north, the pair were kicking their heels rather despondently around Kinloch, banging off at the odd pigeons and rabbits.

"Why don't you," suggested John, "get onto my brother and ask yourselves over for some trout fishing?" As the season had only just opened and the loch unfrozen for only a couple of weeks I could have thought of more amusing pastimes but our frustrated sportsmen were enthusiastic about the idea.

Lou Venables and his friend 'Balloon' Harry are a formidable combination. Lou's business is manufacturing Christmas Cards which he produces in great quantities and Harry as his nickname suggests has a large slice of the balloon market. When they are not attending to these weighty matters they range the countryside together looking for something to shoot or catch and Kinloch is one of their favourite stamping grounds.

They arrived at Rohallion in lively form having lunched well and as eager as anything to have a go at my trout. It was unfortunate that the big boat was having its bottom tarred and only the fibreglass dinghy was available.

When I had bought the dinghy I had been assured that it was completely unsinkable and subsequent hard usage at the hands of the children had proved this to be true. The only thing was that it turned turtle as easily as an eskimo kayak and continued to float equally well either way up. It was alright if you seated yourself centrally and remained still but if you wanted to stand up it was at your peril. Not by any means an ideal fishing boat even for one. For two it was decidedly dodgy.

I explained all this to Lou and 'Balloon' Harry and they appeared to take it in. Just the same I pushed them out from the boat house with some misgiving.

All went well until a couple of hours later I went down to the lochside to tell them that tea was on the table. I found them just coming in to land on the bank below the house. As I watched, 'Balloon' Harry, perched in the bows with the mooring rope in his hand, slowly rose to his feet and prepared to throw the line ashore.

"For God's sake sit down Harry! You'll . . ." but the end of my warning was lost on them. The little boat turned over sharply and Lou and 'Balloon' Harry disappeared from view with landing nets, rods and oars scattered in confusion on the surface of the water. I regret to say that where I should have been deeply concerned that they did not drown or freeze to death in the icy water, I found myself nearly paralysed with laughter.

When I got them back to the house I ransacked my wardrobe to try and find something which might fit them but in the end had to be content with draping them in huge sweaters and trousers about two foot too large round the middle and tied up with string. The idea of tea had been abandoned in favour of something rather stronger and my two absurdly dressed visitors were sitting round the fire when Lou let out an agonised cry. "My clothes. My wet clothes – where are they?"

"I am trying to get them dry on the kitchen stove. Why?" Diana asked.

Lou made a wild rush for the kitchen and came back triumphantly carrying one of the fattest rolls of five pound notes I have ever seen outside of a Bank.

"Thought they might be at the bottom of the loch," he said rather sheepishly.

We tied a long string between the pictures in the drawing room and hung up the notes to dry. Then we turned contentedly to the rapidly disappearing bottle of whisky whilst a small fortune danced before our eyes.

13

WHEN WE first came to Rohallion Jo-Jo was still of nursery school age, Charlie just old enough for the most junior class at the Dunkeld School and Fiona and Neil in more senior classes with their future education still to be decided upon. In those early days Dunkeld was still equipped to educate children right up to school leaving age and we were so happy with the progress of ours that I think we might have been content to have left them there for the whole of their schooling and hope that they might do well enough to get a place at a University. Then by the time Jo-Jo had joined the school and Fiona was nearing the age when a decision would have to be made the matter was taken out of our hands.

It is odd the way authority works. The school had just been newly equipped with workshops, cookery equipment and sewing machines for older boys and girls who wanted to learn a skill, when it was decreed by some remote figure in a Ministry somewhere that the Royal School of Dunkeld which had been turning out good citizens for four hundred years was no longer to be allowed to do so; all the expensive equipment was scrapped and the school redesignated for primary education only.

The traditional village schools in Scotland have over the centuries had a high reputation for producing scholars who in later life make a name for themselves in the professions, arts and industry. Unfortuately these schools have an individuality which is intolerable in the modern State where everything must be streamed and brought down to the lowest common denominator.

Scotland has always been proud of her educational system and the achievements of her sons and it is indeed remarkable how many Scotsmen one finds in high positions all over the world.

There is a story told of a Scottish businessman who decided late in life that the time had come for him to see how the other half lived and accordingly decided to take a business trip to England to see how matters were conducted in that remote country.

On his return he was full of tales of what he had seen and done. Finally one of his listeners asked him what he thought of the English.

"As to that," he said, "I didna meet ony. Ye see I only talked wi' the heids o' departments." A typical Scottish story for we love to poke gentle fun at the Sassenachs.

Now the country schools which have seen the beginnings of so many successful careers are dying out and Royal Dunkeld is only one casualty in the determination of the modern education-alists that all must go the pace of the slowest. The idea that no child should be made to feel that he or she is lagging behind is reflected in the abolition of class marks. Instead the school term report, looked forward to with such trepidation in my young days, is now a wishy-washy affair which grades pupils simply into categories – above average, average, below average, satisfactory or unsatisfactory, shows interest or shows little interest. No longer can the eagle-eyed parent demand to know why his young hopeful has allowed Willie Smith to gain higher marks in arithmetic or note with pride that his offspring is top in English. Now there is no top or bottom – just uniform gradings.

Presumably this is to spare the feelings of the dunces of the class but I never noticed those with low ratings in my school days suffering from maladjustment. On the contrary, they were usually happy-go-lucky chaps with perhaps a compensating ability to play games rather better than their more brainy form mates. My elder brother Gordon, as I recollect, occupied the bottom end of the form during all his time at school and carried the distinction off with the utmost sang-froid, even to the extent of making me feel rather guilty if I got better marks than he did.

At least competitiveness is still not frowned on in the sports field and, as parents, we looked forward to the annual sports day with keen anticipation. I, in particular have a very competitive nature and I would try and impart some of this to my brood, spending much time in explaining that you must get your feet in the corners of your sack to give yourself a chance of winning the sack race and that you must never try to keep your eye on your egg or it would be sure to fall off your spoon in the egg and spoon race.

The great thing about the Dunkeld School sports is that everybody goes in for everything, each class having its own events like three-legged races for the tiny tots to more serious athletics for the bigger children. Apart from class divisions the school is divided into three houses and each competitor wears a ribbon in the appropriate colours of his or her house, every success counting towards the grand total of points recorded on a large blackboard in the middle of the arena.

As the afternoon progresses the tension increases while the marks build up between the houses and there are cheers and counter cheers as each new success is recorded. All in all it is quite an afternoon out and everybody turns up in their best clothes. It might not outdo Ascot but it is still a brave show.

I cannot remember a Sports Day which was spoiled by bad weather but over the years there were some days that I enjoyed more than others.

It was I think our second year at Rohallion when all four children were still at the school which sticks particularly in my mind as one I might have enjoyed better. As usual the weather was fine and warm with high fleecy cloud and just enough wind to rustle the leaves of the trees round the ground. In spite of the children's protests that it would make them a laughing stock, I decided to wear a rather fetching hat I had bought in a moment of weakness from a persistent young Jamaican on the beach at Ocho Rios. It was made entirely of banana leaves and I thought it gave me a look of some distinction. It was however to prove a mistake.

Diana and I had just found an excellent position on the wooden benches nearing the finishing line when John Wilson, the head-master, who was looking around with a rather worried expression at the new arrivals, darted across from the judges' table and clamped his arm on my shoulder.

"Just the very man for the job," he said. "We are short of a judge. With a hat like that you fit the part perfectly."

I glanced at Diana desperately hoping that she would come

up with some suitable excuse but she simply smiled sweetly and said, "I'm sure you'll do it beautifully darling."

Thus it was that instead of being able to enjoy the pleasant afternoon as a spectator, to which I had been looking forward, I found myself in my ridiculous hat grasping one end of the finishing tape. It did not increase my confidence to see that the tape was being held at the other end by my friend Roberto Schiavetta who keeps an excellent fish and chip shop in the High Street but was now also looking distinctly worried at the responsibility which had been thrust upon him.

A moment later the starter's pistol cracked and a gaggle of Primary I six-year-olds were hurtling towards us linked in pairs for the first three-legged race. I was relieved to see that one pair were leading comfortably. One of them was Susan Reid, the eldest daughter of my friends at the Branch Office. They were striding effortlessly for the finishing line when disaster struck. One of the pair got out of step and a moment later they were sprawled on the ground. Unfortunately the two couples behind became hopelessly involved and they too crashed legs and arms sprawling in all directions.

"Atholl!" screamed the partisans as a diminutive couple wearing a yellow sash galloped over the line.

"Get going Susan!" I could hear Cathy Reid shouting alongside Diana and the next three couples scrambled over the line in one horrible heap.

I strode forward and presented the winners with a little red stick which they were to take to the prize table to collect their reward but who was second?

I looked over at Roberto who shrugged his shoulders in an exaggerated gesture of Gallic resignation.

"It was my Florrie was second," shouted a woman from the sidelines.

"No it wis nae. It was oor Effie!" shouted another. Pandemonium reigned and something had to be done. With as much authority as I could muster I gave the yellow stick to the smallest amongst the fallen and the green stick to the other two. I left Susan and her friend out of it. I would be able to square it with them afterwards.

Somebody shouted "Shame!" and I looked over to see Diana, Cathy and Mary eyeing me with baleful stares. Roberto grinned happily. He did not have to hand out the bloody sticks. I was glad to notice that Jo-Jo and her pal Tracy Robertson had untied their handkerchief and were strolling home chattering like magpies and grinning all over their faces. At least they had not been in the hunt and I could not be accused of family favouritism.

Anyone who thinks that judging anything, even if it is only a children's three-legged race, is a piece of cake, is sadly mistaken. During the next hour I went through agonies trying to sort out split decisions. How does one decide that a child who drops her egg a yard from home and then throws herself, egg and all, over the line is less meritorious than the next who has wobbled herself to safety three yards behind? And all the time I was conscious of stony stares from adoring mothers and a sprinkling of antagonistic looking fathers who took everything as seriously as if it had been the Olympics.

Charlie made my task no easier. In the four-legged race he ran like a stag, his hands and toes just touching the ground and his body in a high arch. With his immensely long legs he outdistanced the rest of his class by a full ten yards but when he came to the finishing line he stopped dead. He obviously thought he had won but he had dispensed with the formality of crossing the line.

"Get over the Goddam line!" I shouted at him, forgetting my impartial status while Diana on the touchline shouted, "Go on you fool! Go on!" But Charlie remained rooted to the spot whilst the rest flashed past.

"I giva da race to Charlie," said Roberto.

"But he never crossed the line," I objected to be met with another of Roberto's expressive shrugs, and disqualified him.

In the sack race he was winning again and then with one last hop tumbled to the ground on the wrong side of the winning post. He has a knack of doing things wrong that child, and again I sternly disqualified him.

"That's a shilling you owe me," he announced appearing at my side.

"How do you make that out."

"For the two sixpences I would have won if I had not had my Daddy as a judge."

I settled on the spot, too worn out to argue, and he went off happily to try to satisfy his insatiable capacity for ice-cream. At least that was one problem which was easily solved.

When it came to the more serious events it was obvious that the headmaster had lost any confindence he may have had in me as an official and I was allowed to hand over my office to someone better qualified but my tribulations were not at an end.

John Wilson would not be the excellent headmaster he is without the ability to both coax and intimidate at the same time.

"Assemble at the start line for the father's race," he now announced, fixing me with an imperious eye.

"My heart," I said quickly. "Do you know I have a bad heart. Any sudden exertion and phutt!" I snapped my fingers dramatically.

"Nonsense," said Diana who had appeared from nowhere. "Of course you are to go in for the father's race."

"And you will go in for the mother's race?" I snapped back at her.

"Of course," she replied blandly but I could see that she realised that she had trapped us both.

The father's and mother's races are the highlight at the end of the day. The light relief from the more earnest endeavours of the young.

In deference to weight and age the father's race is a handicap affair and I was relieved to find that I had a good ten yards start on any of the other competitors. My confidence started to surge back. Had I not after all won many a race in my heyday.

"We'll have a pint on which of us finishes ahead," said John Gillies, the taxi driver, as he came up to me dancing on his toes like an entrant for the Powderhall Sprint.

"You're on," I said, "and that goes for any of the rest of you cocky lot." I glared around the circle of grinning faces. At least I could beat a few like Hugh Sim from the garage and Mettick the tailor whom I still owed for a couple of suits.

Of course I think I might have done better if I had not slipped at the start and fallen flat on my face. As it was I finished a discreditable last whilst, it seemed to me, everybody roared their delight at my discomfiture.

Then it was Diana's turn. The ladies as I recollect started level, none of them being willing to admit to greater age or girth. They kicked off their shoes and pulled their tight skirts

130

above their knees whilst the male spectators wolf-whistled their approval.

"I'll back the grey," I shouted and Diana who has had prematurely grey hair since she was twenty, gave me an icy glare.

Then they were off, chins up, arms going like pistons, legs flying while their various offspring raced down the side of the track cheering them on. By half way our Mary had established a commanding lead but then she started to go in the wind and it was Cathy who flashed past the post first, the winner by a comfortable bosom.

After that there was the prize giving, further visits to the ice cream stall and the inevitable frantic search for mislaid articles of clothing before we were able to pack our chattering brood into the car and drive back up the hill.

"Good fun," I said.

"It would have been better if we had had a decent judge," commented Charlie with feeling.

*   *   *

Apart from the various school functions which we attend throughout the year, there are other activities in Birnam and Dunkeld which are generally enjoyed. Of course they are not nearly so varied and sophisticated as those which are available in a large town but not the less worthwhile for that.

There are various bodies like the Women's Rural Institute and the Women's Guild who are assiduous in raising funds for this or that good cause and there is a body called the Wednesday Club which has expanded from its origins as a Church activity to include ladies who are not necessarily regular Church goers. Dull stuff you may think when the town dweller can choose between a discotheque, an X-certificate film or even Bingo any night of the week, but each one to his taste.

I need hardly say that Mary is in the thick of all these activities. 'Jumble' and 'Bring and Buy' sales are food and drink to her but her special interest is reserved for the Wednesday Club. Her enthusiasm for good causes is limitless matched only by her ability to involve others in her schemes so it was with some alarm that we learned one day that she had been elected President of the Club.

131

She did indeed set out on a most ambitious programme but one event which occurred in her year of office and had nothing to do with fund raising, sticks in my mind. She announced it in the most casual way.

"I hope it's a fine day on Saturday," she said.

"What's so special about Saturday?" Diana asked.

"Och, it's just that I'm playing football."

That set us back a bit. I could not have been more surprised if she had suddenly announced that she was taking up skin diving.

We never really got to the bottom of how the whole thing started but it appeared that somewhere along the line the ladies of the Wednesday Club had issued a challenge to the men of the village to a football match.

Being chauvinistically male I was inclined to pooh-pooh the whole idea.

"What are you getting?" I asked. "A ten goal start and a female referee."

"We are playing absolutely level," Mary declared stoutly. "An' what's more we'll give them a thrashing."

"You are on for a pound."

"Twa pun'," said Mary.

It was only after the bet had been struck that a few more details were added.

"Of course," said Mary, "it's only fair that the lassies should wear proper fitba' clothes and the men long dresses and high heeled shoes."

Whichever way the bet went I reckoned this would be worth going to see. Accordingly the whole family were paraded early and, after a brief visit to the Branch Office to get a little inner warmth as a precaution against it turning cold later in the afternoon, we all repaired to the football pitch.

Things were a bit slow in starting. It appeared that there had been some misunderstanding about which sex should use which changing rooms but eventually scattered applause greeted the appearance of the ladies, trotting out very prettily in such a variety of coloured shirts as would have dazzled a blind man. Mary I thought had gone a little too far with a pair of shorts so abbreviated as to be almost invisible under her long jersey.

I could recognise most of the ladies but the men, when they

appeared were a different matter. Who on earth was that one in the bombazine skirt and a couple of balloons stuck under his jumper; or the one with the parasol and the garden party hat?

The game started decorously enough with the men adopting a rather superior attitude, flicking the ball to each other almost contemptuously whilst the opposition ran around widly in circles. It was not long, however, before things started to hot up. I had just picked out Nigel King, our respected factor, heavily disguised in a magnificent lace gown and was pointing him out to Diana when he became the victim of an outrageous assault. He was dribbling nonchalantly down the wing when a maddened lady brought him down with a full blooded rugger tackle and, leaving him floundering on the ground like a dismasted galleon, made off in the opposite direction with the ball.

Archie Macdairmaid, the postie, who had undertaken the role of referee blew his whistle furiously but to no avail. Their blood up, the Amazons bore down on the enemy goal in a flood and by sheer weight of numbers managed to force the ball between the posts. Encouraged by this illegal success they now started to play like a side possessed. Any male coming near the ball was immediately mobbed and borne to the ground, whilst the spectators cheered their heads off. Many a gallant deed was done in their mad delirium. I watched Joan Steel with admiration as she up-ended her six foot three husband from behind and then ran like mad to avoid just retribution whilst her team stormed relentlessly onward.

For a time the men preserved what they could of their dignity but the aggro. eventually became more than flesh and blood could stand. As yet another mêlée took place in mid-field, John Gillies snatched up the ball and sticking it up his jumper ran as fast as his hobble skirt would allow for the enemy goal. It took three of the opposition to bring him down whilst the rest of them, their own transgressions forgotten, screamed for a free kick. Archie, however, had abandoned any hope of either side paying any attention to his whistle and was joining in the game himself. Like all good referees he was quite impartial lending his support to whichever side seemed to be in the most need of assistance.

What any passing motorist on the A.9 must have thought

133

catching sight of some Amazon dashing up the field, 'her' skirts around her thighs or another whose left breast had somehow collapsed in the rough and tumble is hard to imagine. At least it was all lovely fun for the players and spectators.

14

WHEN THE wind blows from the West we lie snugly protected by Rohallion Hill. While the larch trees which form a fringe on the top of Rohallion toss their heads wildly under the onslaught of gales born out of the wastes of the Atlantic Ocean the holocaust passes high over our heads so that a candle flame could burn out of doors without a flicker.

When the wind comes from the North, however, it is a different matter. Then it whips down our little glen seeming to gain in force by being funnelled between the high hills on either side and rattles our shutters with a vengeance. In the morning after a night of wind there are broken branches everywhere and sometimes big trees down across the drive so that we are cut off from the outside world until the woodcutters arrive with their power saws. Even more inconveniently falling branches often bring down our telephone wires making our isolation complete.

It was after one such night of storm that Charlie and I were taking a walk around the house to discover what damage had been done when we came across Freda the swan. She was lying looking bewildered and indignant on the rutted path which leads to the outbuildings at the back of the house. When we approached she arched her neck and hissed at us ferociously but made no attempt to move so that we feared she had a broken leg or even more serious injuries.

Freda was a mute swan, easily identified by her bright orange bill. The mutes are the only swans which winter in Britain and have been known for centuries as royal birds. At one time only the king or such privileged subjects as held a licence from the royal swanherd were allowed to keep swans.

Even today all the swans on the Thames belong either to the Queen or to one or other of two livery companies – the Dyers' and the Vintners'. The livery company birds are distinguished by a distinctive nick made on their beaks whilst the Queen's are unmarked.

Swans because of their great size can be dangerous birds, particularly when they are nesting. A blow from a wing can knock a man down and break bones, so I told Charlie to stand well clear and approached Freda with considerable caution. In fact apart from the furious hissing she offered no resistance when I picked her up in my arms. To my surprise she was quite light. A fully grown mute can weigh up to forty pounds but Freda could scarcely have been half that weight.

We carried her round to the front of the house, rather fearing to take her inside in case she decided to open her great wings and wreak havoc on anything within range. Closer examination proved that our first fears seemed to be unfounded. Legs and wings were intact and I could only assume that she was exhausted from battling with the gale or perhaps had flown into some obstacle in the dark and been temporarily stunned. Now she lay placidly and suffered with dignity close inspection by the rest of the family.

Ever since we had come to Rohallion it had been a matter of regret to me that whilst the Stair Dam at the end of the drive had a swan population none had ever graced our own loch with their presence. True we had many other species of water birds but swans are such satisfyingly majestic birds that I felt they would be a fitting addition to the scenery. Perhaps now if we could nurse Freda back to health she would make our loch her home.

As she seemed quite lively we took her down to the lochside and gently placed her in the water. To our surprise she waggled her tail vigorously, ruffled her wing feathers and struck out with powerful strokes of her webbed feet.

She spent the next few days exploring her new territory, nuzzling around amongst the reed beds at the north end of the loch and fraternising with the ducks, coots and waterhens who swam round and round her like tugs around an Atlantic liner.

Every morning before the children went to school they went down to the water and, calling her name, threw in handfuls of bread and broken biscuits. At first she pretended to take no interest but the moment they had driven off to school she would

make all haste to gobble up their offering. It took a few days for her to get used to this procedure but gradually she lost her shyness and when Charlie and Jo-Jo emerged she would be waiting for them, paddling to and fro a few yards off shore and grabbing at any scraps which were thrown out far enough. After that it was not long before she was practically snatching the food out of their hands. Only if strangers were present at feeding time did she refuse to be tempted inshore.

I really thought Freda had joined our menagerie of semi-tame birds which lived around the house but one day she decided to depart. I was taking my morning walk round the loch with Sara when I heard a loud beating of wings and, peering through the trees, saw her taking off down the loch, her huge wings winnowing the air and her feet furrowing the water. Then she rose majestically into the sky, passing low over the tree tops and, gaining height rapidly, disappeared in the direction of the Tay.

For several days we all waited hopefully for her return but she never came and we feared she had gone off for good to join her own kind out on the estuary.

One morning in the Spring, however, I was sitting at the long table in front of the drawing room window trying to muster my thoughts for the day's stint at the typewriter when two swans came beating their way between the monkey puzzle tree and the tall Cypress and it was obvious that they were heading for the loch. I hurried outside in time to see them landing in a flurry of spray on the far side. One swan looks very much like another to me and we often had casual visitors who stayed a day or two but somehow this time I felt sure that one of them was Freda. I ran into the house for some bread and by the time I came out again they were swimming steadily towards our shore.

"Freda!" I shouted. "Come on Freda!" At once one of them quickened pace and a moment later was greedily stretching out her beak for crusts almost at my feet whilst her companion stood offshore warily ruffling his feathers and swimming to and fro in agitation.

Freda had found herself a mate and had come home.

Within days they were busy constructing a vast nest of sticks and rushes at the end of the loch and the children were instructed to leave them severely alone, apart from resuming the usual feeding routine every morning. It was only after Freda had taken to spending almost all her time sitting on her nest that we ventured to make a closer investigation. To our surprise she showed no signs of resenting our interest even to the extent of allowing us to put our hands under her to see how her laying was progressing. In the end she laid seven eggs and in due course hatched them all successfully. Our bread bill increased sharply when we had nine greedy birds to satisfy every morning and it was late summer before the brood suddenly departed to seek wider horizons.

The presence of Freda and her family had an unexpected effect on the ecology of the loch. At the shallow end they guzzled on the underwater weeds which grew on the muddy bottom. With their sharp bills they cut off more than they could consume with the result that the loose weed floated down to the outlet at the bottom end where it rapidly formed itself into a miniature Sargasso Sea quite ruining one of the best lies for the trout and causing me a great deal of work trying to keep it from damming up the exit completely. I feared too that they would decimate the population of fresh water shrimp and deprive the trout of one of their main sources of food so I was not altogether sorry when they finally departed.

Perhaps fortunately this was not the start of a swannery but I am glad to say that Freda and her mate return faithfully each year to rear the next brood and pay us frequent visits throughout the winter just to see that all is going well at their sanctuary.

*   *   *

I think it was our third summer at Rohallion when we decided that the time had come for Sara to take a husband. For one thing we were beginning to feel guilty of continually having to thwart her amorous ambitions on the grounds of her admirer's unsuitability.

Usually the first indication we got that she was coming into season was the arrival of our friends Jim and Noreen Paton's sheep dog. The Patons have a large farm about three miles away but distance has no meaning in the vocabulary of canine love. Their dog was as fine a fellow as you could wish to see and no doubt a tower of strength when it came to handling sheep but definitely working class and not at all a suitable match for a delicately nurtured young aristocrat – as well as being about three times her size. Alas, Sara had no such reservations and he had only to appear in the vicinity slinking in an underhand way from bush to bush for her to go wild with desire. Doors and windows would have to be bolted and barred and the whole house put in a state of siege whilst every dog for miles around came to join in his vigil.

The decision to provide Sara with a suitable mate entailed much thought and discussion in which the whole family joined. We bought doggy papers to look up kennels advertising their services and talked knowledgeably about strains and pedigrees.

In the end, rather to my relief, it was unanimously decided not to send her to some far distant breeder but to take her to kennels about fifteen miles away where many champions had been produced. On the appointed day we all escorted her to witness the introduction to her husband-to-be. We had to leave her in the kennels for three or four days and we drove home again, feeling rather guilty at abandoning her to an arranged marriage and wondering if after all it might not have been kinder to have let true love have its way.

In the months which followed, Jo-Jo in particular took the closest interest in Sara's condition, even to the extent of making a special calendar to mark off the days. Although she was only six years old she seemed to have a firm grasp of the facts of life without any explanations from us! Disappointingly for her Sara showed few signs of approaching motherhood. I was beginning to have doubts about her pregnancy but Jo-Jo would have nothing to do with such seditious thoughts.

There were still two days to be crossed off on the calendar and we were all sitting round the kitchen table having supper when Sara let out a little whimper and started to turn round and round restlessly in her basket. Jo-Jo darted out of her chair and was just in time to see the first of the litter arrive. Sara had stage managed her big moment to perfection. Two hours later there were six perfect little brown and white puppies squirming around, so small that I could hold them all comfortably in two hands.

From that moment on few mothers could have been more pampered. Even Neil who had hitherto preserved a masculine aloofness from all the fuss took to feeding her with special delicacies and petting her offspring.

I must admit that in breeding from Sara both Diana and I had not been entirely without an ulterior motive. Remembering what we had been told about the demand for King Charles spaniels when we had first bought ours we now looked forward with confidence to making a handsome profit out of her maternal efforts.

When they were nearing six weeks old I declared that it was about time we started to advertise them. The announcement was greeted by the children first with disbelief and then with outrage. By this time each of them had their own favourites which they carried around with them all the time only returning them to the long-suffering Sara for feeding. They messed indiscriminately in the drawing room, the bedrooms and the hall whilst Fiona, Neil, Charlie and Jo-Jo each vehemently denied that their own favourites were responsible.

It was obviously quite an impossible situation to have seven King Charles's running riot round the house so, in spite of all protestations, I firmly put an advertisement in the local paper announcing that we would be prepared to part with pedigreed King Charles pups at 20 guineas each providing that we could be satisfied that they were going to a good home. (No dealers need apply). We then sat back and waited for the rush.

The days and then the weeks passed and nothing happened. We reacted by stepping up our advertising campaign to extravagant heights. Eventually one old lady telephoned to ask if by any chance we had any Cairn Terriers for sale. Diana and I were becoming desperate but the children were delighted.

Fortunately when Ann and Geoffrey Tarlton came up to stay for a few days the puppies proved to be their own best salesmen. They were still just on the young side to leave their mother so we agreed to send their new acquisition down in two weeks' time by air to London where he would be collected and whisked off to a life of luxury in Gloucestershire.

There is a sensible enough regulation on British Airways whereby all dogs must travel in a proper box. The regulation box provided however was also designed to take anything up to a fully grown Alsatian in size and the Tarltons' puppy was so tiny that it seemed rather absurd for him to occupy so much space. The Captain of the aircraft allowed him to travel on his escort's knee in the cabin. The result was that when the aircraft landed at Heathrow we received a telephone call to say that not only one of the passengers but the Captain himself wanted puppies.

After that it seemed suddenly that everyone wanted them so that it was with relief tinged with sadness that we saw the last one depart as a companion to an autistic child. We were later to hear from the parents that the two were inseparable and that the child's condition had taken a considerable turn for the better since getting her pet so, if our financial ambitions had not been entirely realised, we felt that Sara's efforts had added to the sum of human happiness.

The breeding habits of our cat population, which I have already mentioned, ebbed and flowed to such an extent that we scarcely ever knew how many there were on the ration strength.

I have a firm conviction that cats should be made to work for a living and are much happier if they do. I made it a general rule therefore that all cats should be put out at night and this policy was shown to pay dividends by the number of mice and rats which were brought to the back door as offerings from time to time. It had the disadvantage on the other hand of making it difficult to know exactly how we stood at any given time.

One of our greatest characters was a large tom cat who was pure white except for a black patch over one eye and inevitably christened Nelson.

Nelson was a great hunter and would disappear for perhaps a week, scorning domestic comforts and then, for no reason take to spending days on end asleep in front of the kitchen stove, waking up only to be fed. His appetite for female company rivalled his prowess as a hunter but he was a considerate lover. Where he found his brides I cannot imagine but his habit was to bring them home and install them in a comfortable outhouse where they would inevitably produce a litter.

There are few more endearing creatures than tiny kittens and to begin with we used to adopt them with enthusiasm, rear them carefully and then try to find suitable homes for them. We stuck notices in shop windows in the village and the children assiduously canvassed their friends at school, but so great was

Nelson's production that it was not long before the local demand was satiated.

Eventually we were driven to giving them to the pet shop in Dundee but we always had the nagging feeling that in spite of the care taken by the owners of the shop to find good homes for them there would inevitably be some which would add to the city's already large population of strays. We eventually did what we should have done much sooner and took Nelson to be doctored. Alas, he took this act of treachery so badly that soon afterwards he left home for good.

This was not to be the end of our troubles. Nelson's harem, either for sentimental reasons or from force of habit, continued to look upon Rohallion as a maternity home. Their efforts to combine the comforts of Rohallion with freedom from interference were ingenious and varied but the prize for ingenuity must go to an unnamed tortoiseshell who had her litter in a bird nesting box we had erected on a tall pole outside the kitchen window. Unaware that she was being observed from inside the house, she would approach her unusual nursery with exaggerated caution. Then with a sudden rush she would shoot up the ten foot pole and with a display of extraordinary gymnastic ability hang on with her hind legs, lean over backwards with her fore paws threshing the air wildly until she got a grip on the edge of the seed tray, and haul herself over the ledge. It was only when the kittens reached the weaning stage that she discovered to her chagrin that there was no way of getting them down to earth short of their growing wings. We duly came to her rescue. Then she disappeared with her young into the bushes and we never saw them again.

With the passing of the years however the outside cat population has dwindled and we again have two neutered inside cats called Wishy and Washy whose appetites are only excelled by their idleness. They sleep their lives away comfortably in front of the kitchen stove while the mice play around them and Mary has been driven back to her role of mouse trapper in chief.

15

I do not understand television any more than I understand the telephone or the radio or even the motor car. I just take them for granted but sometimes I feel I would be just as happy without instantaneous communications and doing my shopping in the village with a pony and trap.

"You want to get in on the television scene," kind friends are constantly advising me. "That is where the real money is. Surely you can do better than all that rubbish we have to put up with."

Although I watched and applauded the efforts of my friends on the medium it was something I never felt I could come to grips with.

Then one day my friend Keith Richardson of Yorkshire Television rang to say he wanted to come and see me with a proposition. The excitement before his arrival was intense. Surely this was to be the big opportunity and he would offer me the chance of creating a new series which would catapult me to fame and fortune overnight.

Alas when he arrived it transpired that he was not in the least interested in my literary skill. It happened that he was helping to make a film series called 'Hadleigh' and the script took them to Germany for one episode. The financial powers had decided that with the poor rate of exchange this was altogether too expensive a venture and Keith had been charged with finding an alternative. Rohallion he had decided looked sufficiently like a small German castle to serve the turn. And so it came about.

Of course there was considerable excitement in our quiet little community at the imminent arrival of such well known stars as Gerald Harper and Eric Pohlmann – and it was not bad for business either.

The evening of Keith's arrival happened to coincide with the opening of a new hotel in Birnam so we took Keith along with us. Ladyhill is not really a rival to the Branch Office. Peter and Sybilla Munro have set out to provide a small luxury hotel specialising in good food where, wonderful to relate in our part of the world, you can get a meal up to ten o'clock at night. It so impressed Keith that he booked the whole place for his film unit so Ladyhill House got off to a good start. Then there were other locations to be found involving the payment of fees and even the Cathedral Restoration fund benefited from giving permission for the unit to film its venerable walls.

Our children of course took the closest interest in all that was going on with Joanna in particular ingratiating herself in the most shameless way with the Director and Producer in the naive belief that she might be allowed to appear on the screen. Neil who had already taken over three rooms at the back of the house to indulge his interest in making stereophonic equipment was absorbed in the technical side of the operation but this did not inhibit his love of practical jokes.

On the day shooting was due to commence Neil had resurrected an old canvas-backed chair from the summer house and painted 'Director' on the back in the approved Hollywood style. The Director, Derek Bennett, graciously accepted this offering but when he came to sit in it it immediately collapsed while Neil fell about laughing.

By and large however everything went well. For my part I began to understand for the first time what television was all about. After each day's shooting was over we would repair to Ladyhill and in that hospitable atmosphere I was able to improve my education on a subject on which I had hitherto been so lamentably ignorant.

Matters might have rested there but for another twist of fate in which Rohallion again played a part.

Normally I do not go a bundle on other writers. The daily stint at the typewriter satisfies my literary ambitions more than adequately without my wanting to get involved in talking shop out of working hours. There are of course exceptions to this generality as Charles will testify. Once a gushing visitor said to him, "It must be lovely to have a father who is a writer. I don't think I have ever met anyone who has written a book before."

"I don't think I've ever met anyone who hasn't," Charles replied gloomily.

One of a number of exceptions to my wariness of fellow writers is Charles MacHardy who lives in Dundee and has written such best sellers as "Send down a Dove" and "The Ice Mirror".

On one occasion I met Charles in a well-known Dundee establishment called "The Howff" and found him in a despondent frame of mind.

"I can't get on with my book living in a city like Dundee. There are too many distractions," he complained. "I am going to get away for a few months. Drop out in the country until I get the damn thing finished."

"Good idea." I said. "Where were you thinking of going?"

"Rohallion," he said.

And did.

The Hadleigh incident had half persuaded me that I might have a go at a T.V. script and I consulted Charles. He's a useful ideas man. It was he who suggested that I meet a producer he knew in London. Knowing Charles I was not surprised when the producer turned out to be a very attractive young lady.

Christine Fox is not only attractive but almost alarmingly intelligent. As luck would have it she was in the middle of producing a new series with Dave Allen, the Irish comedian and was coming to Scotland in search of material. Dave was taking a break from telling Irish jokes and was putting together a programme wandering round the country chatting up interesting characters.

It so happened that Jo-Jo was having a belated birthday party and had about twenty-five school friends for tea. As a surprise we had laid on, of all things, a circus.

This perhaps requires some explanation. I have a friend called "Fire Clouds" who runs, and is one half of the cast of, what he proudly calls "The Smallest Circus in the World". Few would dispute the claim. He is the Ring Master and Fire Eater. His partner Yo-Yo is the clown. They are supported by one dog, four turtle doves, a snake, a tortoise and a rabbit. They tour small halls all over Scotland to the immense enjoyment of their young audiences.

When I told Christine this any hope I had of using her to further my T.V. ambitions went out of the window. All she wanted to do was to have Dave Allen interview Fire Clouds and be part of the audience at Jo-Jo's party.

Fortunately it turned out a lovely sunny afternoon. Neil fixed up a discotheque on the terrace and whilst all the children were jigging around to the music, the circus was getting ready down by the boathouse and Christine's television crew were setting up their cameras.

The faces of the young guests when they found themselves on television with a real live clown, a top-hatted 'ring-master' and Dave Allen were a joy to behold. It did nothing however to satisfy my own growing ambition to get into this magical world where it seemed so much easier to earn a crust than toiling away at the typewriter.

Like most other writers I had appeared from time to time on the box talking about books and so on. It was hardly what one might call a creative activity but it was after one of these programmes that my next major involvement with the medium took place. The interview took place at Rohallion and again the old house worked its magic. A few days later Scottish Television rang up to say that they wanted to do a film of my life style – in which of course Rohallion was to play an important part. If I could not write for television here at least was a chance of acting on it – even if the role I was playing was only myself.

Once again Rohallion became the scene of intense activity. There seemed to be lights and cameras and wires everywhere. Best of all from the children's point of view was that they were all to appear. There were shots of them being taken to school, boating on the loch, rambling across the hillside etc. I was also to be seen working at my typewriter, fishing, shooting and so on. It was altogether a hilarious business which we all thoroughly enjoyed under the benign direction of Ted Williamson.

When it came to doing the bit about game shooting I had the greatest difficulty in convincing Ted that it was difficult to produce pheasants to order in front of the cameras and to add to this was the additional complication that they were out of season. It so happened that one of my neighbours, John Forsyth whom I had invited to take part in a mock shoot arrived with a dead pigeon in the back of his Land Rover. By dint of letting off our guns and then having the dogs retrieve the pigeon we managed to simulate some action but I could see that Ted was hankering for something a little less artificial.

Right at the end of the session we were all walking down a hill track with the cameraman lying on the path filming our progress when one of the dogs put up a rabbit out of a ditch and, pouncing after it, grabbed it literally inches from the lens of the camera. Ted was delighted but when next day we got the report of the rushes from Glasgow there was a note saying that the shooting of the pigeons was fine but the gimmick with the rabbit did not ring true!

For Jo-Jo the greatest moment of all came when at the end of the film the whole family were to be pictured sitting round the big fireplace in the drawing room playing various games. Jo-Jo reckoned that whichever child happened to be playing back-gammon with me would hog most of the camera. "Why don't we draw lots who's to play with you Daddy?" she suggested and a moment later arrived with a cup full of folded slips of paper. To nobody's surprise the first name out of the cup was Jo-Jo but unfortunately for her I quickly picked a second slip which bore the same name! – and so did all the others! For this bit of deceit she was banished to play Mastermind with Diana but filming was held up for fully ten minutes whilst she got over this miscarriage of her plot.

"She certainly has the temperament of a film star," said Ted as he patiently coaxed her back to a better humour.

It was after this adventure that Robin Crichton of Edinburgh Films came up with the idea that he and I should do a docu-mentary on the Scots enjoying themselves and so for the first time I was given the chance of trying my hand at script writing. I may say it was a hand which was firmly held by Robin himself but at least it was a start and again the beginning and the end of the film was set at Rohallion. In between times the camera wandered to Highland Games, football matches, Bingo halls, pleasure steamers and even a strip club. The last scene before the wind-up had me with my trousers rolled up to the knee squelching through the mud in the direction of Ireland inter-viewing competitors at the Palneckie flounder festival where people come from far and near to try and catch flounders with their bare feet! By the end of it all I really had begun to feel like a seasoned performer but I am under no illusion that the real star was dear old Rohallion.

151

16

THE FURTHER you get from London the more neighbourly people become. Or so it has always seemed to me. Perhaps it is not really so and it is only that the quality of friendship is different. I lived happily in London for a great number of years and had a large circle of acquaintances but few really close friendships. By close friendships I mean those where one can drop unceremoniously into each other's houses, watch the children growing up and share our hopes and fears. There were so many people in London whom I met almost daily over the years in the office or my club or in some regularly used bar and with whom I had the closest rapport but whose private lives were a closed book. One knew vaguely that they lived in Kensington or Esher or Balham, that they had wives with whom they did or did not get on and children in various stages of growth but the background remained shadowy and unreal.

There were, of course, others not often connected with one's daily routine to whose parties one was asked and whom one duly asked back to some entertainment of one's own but somehow the social round was even more remote in terms of real friendship. The brittle conversation which is the stuff of cocktail and dinner parties is unrewarding in terms of human relationship.

In a big city, despite the multitude of diversions it has to offer, the greatest enemies are boredom and loneliness. By contrast Diana and I once lived for a year on one of the more remote of the Orkney Islands where the days were never quite long enough to fit in all we wanted to do and the feeling of being part of a community was very real.

Rohallion has a similar effect on us. With fewer artificial distractions people become more important in one's life. When new people move into the area they are at first the subject of absorbed speculation even to the point of inquisitiveness until they become familiar friends. Everyone's business is everyone's business. We soon found it was impossible to do the simplest thing without someone making a comment about it.

"Did you enjoy your lunch at Timothy's yesterday?" somebody would ask who so far as we knew did not even have reason to know we had been into Perth. Somebody else would have seen our car sitting outside the restaurant and thought it interesting enough to report.

There are, of course, many people who, accustomed to the anonymity of city life, would find this an intolerable intrusion upon their privacy. Personally I do not and indeed find great amusement in it particularly when the bush telegraph gets it all wrong.

There was one occasion which I particularly enjoyed. It happened that Diana was away on one of her rare visits to London on her own and I was driving over to lunch with my mother at Kinloch when my car broke down right outside Ann and Peter Stock's house. There was nobody at home but the door was open so I went in, helped myself to a large gin and rang my brother John to come and pick me up.

Ann Stock, I should mention here, is a particularly attractive and desirable young woman and it so happened that her husband Peter was also away for a few nights on business. It was three days before John Young got around to towing my car into the garage and all that time it sat on the main road by Ann's front gate.

It proved too much even for Derek who whilst priding himself on knowing everything that is going on is the soul of discretion.

"For Heaven's sake get your car moved," he said to me behind his hand one morning. "Every old tabby in the village is saying that Diana has run off with Peter and that you've moved in with Ann!"

It was too good an opportunity to miss. Next morning I waited until the bar at the Branch Office was comfortably full before I walked in with Ann. In the hush which followed I said to Derek in a loud voice.

"Ah, Derek, you know my mistress I believe!"

I am happy to say that several people choked on their beer

and I left rapidly but it was quite a time before Ann forgave me.

I myself am a great gossip but I hope not a malicious one. I think most people if they would admit it are intensely interested in what everybody else is up to and this is particularly true in the country where everyone is bound together by a community of interest. You do not have to be a farmer to want to know what so and so got for his cattle in the market or a fisherman to enjoy hearing who has caught what on the various beats of the Tay. It may indicate an idle mind but to me it is one of life's little enjoyments.

It is largely during the long winter months when the harvest is safely in, the tourists long departed and the curtains drawn by teatime to shut out the night, that the social life of the countryside gets underway. It is nothing if not varied – functions in the village hall, high tea with a neighbouring farmer and a game of pontoon for pennies or grander occasions when one is expected to change for dinner and play bridge for high stakes. There are subscription balls for which the very grand people lend their castles and everyone wears Highland evening dress, and more modest private affairs where the young happily dance until dawn whilst their elders seek out a quiet corner to while away the night in companionable conversation.

Then of course there are the shooting parties which for me are a particular delight. When I was a boy shooting was not the expensive business it is today. Every day of our school holidays when we could escape from parties to which our parents would insist on taking us in the mistaken belief that we would have fun, my brother and I would spend either shooting or fishing according to the season of the year. The young of today do not have the same opportunities unless their fathers happen to own a big estate and even then many estates are let to syndicates in order to make ends meet and the day of the small rough shoot is almost over. Shooting today is big business.

All the ground round Rohallion is let to an American firm with international ramifications who think nothing of flying their executives or favoured customers over from the States for a few days 'huntin'. No expense is spared. The guests are supplied with guns and cartridges and even fitted out with shooting clothes so that at the start of a shoot the room reserved for them at the headkeeper, Tom Wilkie's, house looks like a sports outfitters as the guests kit themselves out with shooting boots, waterproof trousers and jackets. Then Tom reads them a stern lecture on the need to observe safety precautions before they all pile into Land Rovers and set off for the first drive.

Tom's lecture is not a formality. On one occasion when I was asked to join them I sat next to one of the American guests in a Land Rover and, feeling the need to make some sort of polite conversation, asked him how he liked the 'over and under' twelve bore with which he had just been issued.

"I don't rightly know pal," he said cheerfully. "I guess this is the first time I've ever had a weapon in my hands in my life!"

As luck would have it I was drawn next to him in the line. For the first few drives I was much more worried than the pheasants need have been as they streamed untouched over his head!

Just the same they are a cheerful and hospitable lot and, whilst there are some who add little to the bag there are others who have developed into reasonably good shots.

Fortunately for me there are still quite a few shoots close by which are privately run and to which I am lucky enough to be asked. To my mind there is no pleasanter or more relaxing way of spending a day. At the same time I am aware that there is a considerable body of opinion which regards all blood sports with horror even to the extent of objecting to the catching of a few trout on a quiet summer's evening. No doubt many of them are inspired by genuine if misguided humanitarianism. Few take the trouble to learn anything about the subject on which they are so vocal. Others deliberately distort the facts claiming that tyrannical landlords clear their lands to make way for pheasants and grouse with a few other absurdities thrown in for good measure.

The most vehement of the critics are those whose whole view on life is contorted by class hatred and they find blood sports a convenient stick with which to beat the objects of their envy and malice. Incomplete people, really to be pitied rather than condemned.

Shooting is very much part of the countryman's everyday life whether he lives in a cottage or a castle. It is a pity that it has become so expensive that fewer and fewer are able to enjoy a day's sport at the partridges or pheasants but many landowners are not averse to giving permission to shoot rabbits or pigeons particularly to their tenants, and beaters, who before the war might earn half a crown a day, can now expect something like five pounds for the next best way of participation short of actually shooting.

My enthusiasm for shooting however does not blind me to some of the more unfortunate trends which have been developing to a marked extent since the war. The most unacceptable aspect from the countryman's point of view is the acquisition of large estates by men who have made a lot of money suddenly and want to try and buy their way into social acceptability. Many of them are absentee landlords, leaving it to others to make for them the maximum return on their investment and only appearing with their guests at infrequent intervals to show off their grouse moors or their pheasant coverts or their salmon fishings.

Scotland has always suffered to a certain extent from these unwanted invaders but nowadays it seems that there is hardly a place that comes onto the market that does not fall into the 'wrong' hands. Then the trouble starts. Tenants established for generations find themselves replaced or rack-rented, rights of way disappear and notices threatening dire penalties for trespass grow up like mushrooms.

I once attended a shoot where one of these new estate owners had been asked as a guest by his reluctant neighbour. His loudly voiced opinions on everything under the sun from his newly acquired knowledge on how to breed pheasants to his undoubtedly authoritative pronouncements on how to avoid income tax did nothing to endear him to his host or his fellow guests so that I for one found it hard to conceal my delight when, negotiating a barbed wire fence, he tore the seat out of his immaculately tailored breeches revealing a delicious pair of powder blue pants underneath. The climax of a miserable day for him came when, unloading his gun behind his Rolls Royce Corniche, he managed somehow to let off both barrels at once into the back tyre.

Such disclosures however are unworthy of one for whom the bonhomie and the good-fellowship of a shooting party are almost as enjoyable as the sport itself. As I have said, shooting parties are one of the recurring delights of my life at Rohallion as one season follows another. Charlie is also infected by the bug and I take him whenever I can to stand with me in the grouse butts or at the pheasant pins. Soon he will be old enough to be armed with a light gun. Then perhaps he will realise that it is not so easy as it looks and stop exclaiming in disgust each occasion I register a miss. I only hope that by the time he is grown up it will not be a thing of the past.

Where the expense of rearing pheasants and partridges (without which they would be very soon threatened with extinction), and the cost of laying on a shoot is rapidly making it impossible except for the very rich, the same cannot be said of fishing. Certainly salmon fishing is the exception with the high prices which are being paid for a week on a good stretch, but trout fishing is, at least theoretically, free in Scotland. With certain exceptions the only way to stop someone fishing your water is to prosecute for trespass and even this presents technical difficulties.

This peculiarity of Scottish law was borne in on me rather painfully when one year I shared with Derek in renting a salmon beat on the Tay. One would be in process of enjoying a quiet day at the riverside with friends when a bus would draw up and out would troop thirty of forty burly coal miners. Without so much as the courtesy of bidding you "Good Morning" they would line the river bank and thrash away enthusiastically. I got the distinct feeling that at the slightest protest we would be likely to finish up alongside the fish.

At the same time there are many fishermen who politely ask for permission to fish a remote loch only to be abruptly refused by the landlord or his agent. As in many cases the landlord himself only fishes the loch at best seldom, this too is not the right way of going about things.

In fact there is trout fishing in plenty for all without trampling on other people's rights. The big landlords with fishing to spare should encourage the formation of fishing clubs and place the onus of preserving and stocking the water on the members. I recollect Michael Scott who is agent for the Countess of Sutherland's considerable estates in the north, doing just this when he was having a lot of trouble with poachers. When he gave them their own loch the erstwhile poachers turned enthusiastic gamekeepers and everyone lived happily ever after.

On my own loch, small though it is, I readily give permission for anyone to fish who has the courtesy to ring up and only insist that they leave a record of their catch for my game book.

The truth is that most Scottish lochs are grossly underfished with the result that there are too many small trout who never grow to any great size. Dunkeld is lucky in having its own well-run fishing club where for a modest subscription members have access to both salmon and trout fishing on good stretches of the Tay and the Braan as well as several lochs. They also see to it that poaching is at a minimum.

When I was younger my brother Gordon and I were not above a little poaching ourselves. As a man of the hills Gordon has a great knowledge of some of the more remote lochs which were usually stacked with trout. Our expeditions were made at night, trampling sometimes many miles over the moors to spend the hours of darkness by the waterside. Moonlight nights were the best when one could cast one's line where the moon shone on the water and see where the flies were landing.

For the keen fisherman I will give away a secret here. Between us we perfected a fly made from the wing feathers of an owl which we fished dry. The fine texture of the feathers made the fly seem to shimmer on the surface of the water and it proved absolutely deadly and, at risk of being accused of telling a fisherman's story I must relate how three of us – the third was the local policeman – fared on one famous evening with our patent fly.

We had chosen a loch high up in the hills which Gordon reported from previous experience to be full of great trout. We did not start fishing until close on midnight and it soon became obvious that this was to be a night to end all nights. Conditions were perfect and with almost every cast we hooked a fish and they were averaging well above a pound.

With dawn breaking we struggled down the mountainside to where we had left the car by a fast running stream. There we brewed up some coffee and laid our catch out in rows on the bank. They numbered a hundred and ten and weighed a hundred and thirty pounds.

As we sat gazing at them we were alarmed to hear the noise of a vehicle coming up the hill track and before we could do anything about hiding our catch it bounced into view. Fortunately it turned out to be another party of fishermen from Dundee who had come up to fish the stream. Now they gazed in open-mouthed amazement at the catch laid out before them. Little thinking that we had spent the night on the hidden loch they asked how we had come by such a miraculous haul.

No fisherman likes to give away his secrets to a stranger and Gordon was equal to the occasion.

"Ah," he said, "you have to get up early and look under the flat stones."

I hope Derek will not mind my retailing another poaching story which concerns one of his customers, who shall remain nameless but who pays him a visit from time to time. He is a charming Irishman and I spent one evening with him happily talking about fishing. It soon became obvious to me that he had a close acquaintance with most of the best beats on the Tay.

We were well down the bottle when he said to me casually, "Would you care to come for a bit of salmon fishing with me tomorrow."

"I would be delighted to," I replied and not being sure to which beat he was inviting me asked whether I should bring long or short waders.

"Surr," he said, "when you come fishing with me you chust wear your running shoes!"

17

WHEN I was a boy Christmas was not regarded in Scotland as a time for celebration. Indeed for most Scotsmen it was not even a holiday. Farm workers had only one day's holiday a year and that was New Year's Day and New Year is still the real time for serious celebration. Now however we Scots have also adopted Christmas so the whole business starts on Christmas Eve and carries on until past New Year's Day, it being scarcely worth while breaking off the festivities for the week that separates them.

In self defence we try to keep our Christmas at Rohallion an entirely family affair but at the same time we take it very seriously. Weeks before Christmas pies and puddings and cakes are ordered from Miss Milne's bakery in Birnam, Bert Wood earnestly consulted about turkeys and hams whilst each year a new hiding place is found where early presents can be concealed from prying eyes.

For a fortnight before the great day Rohallion is a house of secrets. When it is considered that each of the six of us has presents to buy for each of the others without giving any inkling of his plans it will be realised that the clandestine expeditions to the shops and the subsequent security measures try our ingenuity to the utmost. If James and Adam, my two boys by a previous marriage whom I have not mentioned in this book for fear of confusing the reader, are to be with us the task is made even more complicated. Then there are Mary's three offspring, Phillip, Maureen and Joyce, my brother's family over at Kinloch, my mother and sister-in-law Patricia and so on and on until the whole thing is apt to assume the overtones of a nightmare.

It is not really until the fifteen foot Christmas tree is in its place reaching up the well of the circular staircase and decorated with cottonwool snow, glitter, coloured balls and fairy lights that we begin to get filled with the Christmas spirit and actually look forward to the day.

Even the older children do not forgo the traditional stocking at the end of their beds so Diana and I spend Christmas eve closeted in the drawing room from which everyone else is banned as we fill stockings and wrap last minute presents. Then after all the young have gone to reluctant bed we pile the parcels under the tree and pour ourselves a strong nightcap to celebrate the miracle that our finances have stood the strain for yet another year.

Christmas morning is the time for strict discipline if all our plans are not to be disrupted. At what seems an unearthly hour our bedroom is invaded by the whole family including Sara while stockings are opened. Then we troop down to breakfast but the tree must not be touched until all the breakfast things are washed up and put away. Then the rule is that only one present at a time is allowed to be opened to be admired by all before the next one is given out. Lists are made so that the right person can be thanked for the right present and a huge box provided for discarded wrappings.

All this takes a considerable time so that it is almost midday before the ceremony has been completed. Then it is time for my mother, traditionally our only guest, to arrive. She comes booming through the front door like a galleon in full sail bearing with her her own gifts and presents from other members of the family and the whole business starts all over again. Fortunately she is always under the impression, which is not entirely errone-ous, that we are on the brink of bankruptcy so tucked away amongst the gaily wrapped parcels there are more practical items like brandy for the Christmas pudding and a bottle of gin for immediate consumption.

Christmas lunch is a prolonged affair and it is late afternoon before the last crackers are pulled and the port passed on its final round. Then it is feet up around a roaring log fire whilst the younger ones disappear to various parts of the house to play with their new presents.

This quiet domestic scene is however something of an oasis of peace in the turbulent days which follow leading up to a peak of frenzied celebration on New Year's Eve. Each year, like that resolution to give up smoking every time the price goes up, we resolve to lock all the doors and go to bed early so that the first day of the New Year will see us bright-eyed and hearty whilst the rest of the population stumble around like boxers about to be counted out. Each year we fail lamentably to carry out our resolution. There are two basic approaches to a Scottish New Year. The first is to lay in a massive stock of whisky, leave the front door open and the lights all ablaze and wait for the neighbours to beat a path to your door. The second is to become a nomad oneself, travelling from house to house with a bottle of whisky in your back pocket with which to toast the health of your various hosts.

The great moment is of course when midnight strikes and you join hands with whoever you are with to sing Auld Lang Syne before the bottles start to circulate again even more furiously.

For our part Diana and I usually join a dinner party which John gives at Kinloch every year and then let the events of the evening take care of themselves. One of these celebrations in particular sticks in my mind. John's New Year's Eve party by tradition has at least a couple of Africans as guests. They are sent to him by the Victoria League amongst whose many good works is the finding of homes to offer hospitality to overseas students who are unable to return to their own countries.

This particular night I was seated next to an enormous African whose name I only remember as Solomon. In the course of the meal I tried to explain to him the peculiarly Scottish custom of 'first footing'. It is considered lucky in Scottish households that the first person to set foot over the threshold in the New Year should be a tall, dark and preferably handsome man and he should bear with him as tokens of prosperity for the following year something to drink, something to eat and something to burn. Whilst I was telling Solomon of our custom it suddenly occurred to me that here was surely the perfect 'first foot'. Why did he not accompany us on our rounds that night? Solomon's white teeth flashed in an enormous grin. "Well I may not be handsome," he said, "but I sho' is dark."

We armed him with a bottle of whisky, a kipper and a lump of coal and set off in the direction of my other brother Gordon's house up the glen. On the way we passed a house where all the windows were a blaze of light. It belonged to a friend of Gordon's, Major Aldo Campbell, and we decided that he should be our first victim.

We sent Solomon, bearing his gifts up the driveway ahead of us while we crouched in the bushes. Solomon pressed the bell and Aldo himself answered the door.

"I'se yoh first foot," we heard Solomon boom holding up the kipper between a finger and thumb. For a moment we thought the gallant Major was going to have a fit. His eyes bulged and his lips moved soundlessly. I think he might even have slammed the door had not Diana and I rushed forward to save the situation. He told me afterwards that all he could hear was a disembodied voice and see the whites of Solomon's rolling eyes.

It was several hospitable whiskies later before we escaped from Aldo's party and went in search of the next one. I am certain that some of the hill crofts we visited had never seen a full-blooded African in the flesh before and I'm not sure who enjoyed the experience more, the victims of our joke or Solomon himself.

Dawn was already breaking over the hills before we finally made our way homeward.

The last we saw of Solomon he was weaving his way upstairs to bed, shaking his curly head and muttering, "Yoh Scots are crazy, crazy peoples."

*   *   *

We have now been at Rohallion for ten years but that is the merest blink of an eye in its history. Only the other day I received a letter from a lady with an exhaustive knowledge of Scottish history. Did I know the origin of the name Rohallion? It was something I had asked all manner of people since we had come to the house but had never found the answer.

Now I learned that it is one of only three places in the whole of Scotland which perpetuate the tribal name for the ancient Caledonians who roamed the hills three thousand years ago. The name for the Caledonians was Chaillean so that Dunkeld was originally Dun-Chaillean – the township of the Caledonians. That great mountain Schiehallion was Sidh Chaillean – the fairy hill of the Caledonians, a description which anyone who has climbed it would agree with and lastly Rohallion, the Rath of the Caledonians.

The Scottish National Dictionary defines a Rath or Raith as "a circular earthwork, a hill fort" and the authority George Chalmers wrote in 1807 "The chieftains ruled their territories from their raths or fortified villages."

So long before Sir William Stewart came to build his hunting lodge people lived here under the shelter of the same hills and looked up at the same stars. Indeed it is likely that Sir William built on the site of an existing cottage. Violet Jacobs, that most neglected of Scottish poets, wrote of Rohallion when it must have been only a shepherd's croft set by the side of the loch:

ROHALLION

Ma buits[1] are at rest on the midden,
I haena a plack;[2]
Ma breeks are no dandy anes, forrit,
And waur at the back;
On the road that comes oot o' the Hielands
I see as I trayvel the airth
Frae the braes at the back of Rohallion
The reek[3] abune Perth.

There's a canny wee hoose wi' a gairden
In a neuk o' Strathtay;
Ma mither is baking the bannocks,
The weans are at play;
And at gloaming my feyther, the shepherd,
Looks doon for a blink o' the licht
When he gaithers the yowes[4] at the shieling
Tae fauld[5] them at nicht.

There isna a hoose that could haud me
Frae here tae the sea
When a wind frae the braes o' Rohallion
Comes creeping tae me;

1. boots 2. halfpenny 3. smoke 4. ewes 5. pen

And never a lowe frae the ingle
Can draw like the trail an' the shine
O' the stars i' the loch o' Rohallion
A fitstep o' mine.

There's snaw i' the wind, an' the weepies[6]
Hang deid on the snaw,
An' pale the leaves left on the rowan,
I'm soothward awa';
But a voice like a wraith blaws ahint me
And sings as I'm lifting my pack,
"I am waiting – Rohallion, Rohallion –
Ma lad, ye'll be back!"

6. A weed known as 'Stinkin' Georgie'

So many people must have set out from Rohallion in its
many disguises to seek their fortunes, and have had reason to
remember it with nostalgia. Now another generation is about to
take wing. Fiona is in her second year reading law at Aberdeen
University and Neil who for the past eighteen months has been
creating more and more elaborate Hi-Fi equipment which flows
into every room in the house, plans to spend a year working in a
factory before also going to Aberdeen to take a degree in
engineering, Charlie is boarding up at Aberfeldy and is showing
great promise as an artist and only Jo-Jo is still with us all the
time. The other day we were proudly relating the achievements
of our family to a visitor whilst Jo-Jo listened solemnly.
    "And what are you going to do, Jo-Jo?" she asked her.
    "Ah dinna ken," Jo-Jo said in her incredible Scottish accent.
"I think they must have run oot of brains when they came to
me." Soon she too will be going away to board and Diana and I
will be alone in the big house, keeping it warm for any of them
who want to return for a spell.
    There are other changes taking place around us like the new
road to the north which will now run a mile further away from
our gates and bypass Dunkeld, so that I will no longer hear the
lorries climbing the hill. The little family grocer in Birnam where
we used to do most of our shopping is now a Spar Store and my
friend Bob Miller, the chemist, has changed himself for some

reason to being the only ironmonger I know who also sells ice-cream. To my great joy Jenny Mitchell whose mother runs the Dunkeld House Hotel has come home with her husband from London to open a fine bookshop where they humour me by displaying copies of my books in the window and add considerably to the cultural life of the village.

Another effect of the new road has already been that the arena where the Birnam Games were held has now disappeared under asphalt and concrete but, after missing a year, another site has been found and they were held again last summer more successfully than ever.

Derek has moved to a fine house up on the hill above the village where he monopolises all the local labour in making improvements so that I can no longer get anything done at all at Rohallion. Peter the Provost has retired from clambering over roofs and Stewart Robertson no longer sets off in the small hours of Monday morning for Oban.

But there are many things which do not change. I know for a certainty that if I call in at the Branch Office on a Thursday Freddie Townsley will already be in his corner seat at the bar. Freddie is the butler at one of the large houses in the district but he is also my racing adviser. Between us we have pulled off many a fine win against the bookies. When there is a local race meeting at Perth Fred always comes with us but at first I noticed that we were not really very successful. It was not until I observed a strange phenomenon that matters improved. It was that if Fred suggested a horse to me and then also backed it himself it always lost. If he backed something else mine won. Working on this principle at one meeting I insisted that he backed none of the tips he gave me. Result: I had six winners and my racing adviser, of course, six losers.

As I write these final words a great party is being planned at Rohallion for Fiona's twenty-first birthday.

I hope my daughter Carol will be there with her husband and James who is learning to be a ballet dancer with the Rambert School of Ballet and Adam who plans to be a doctor. It will probably be the last time the whole family will be under our roof together. There will be eighty young people who plan to dance the whole night through.

Last night dusk did not start to fall until after eleven o'clock and the heat of the long day of sunshine still lingered on. Neil had moved his huge loudspeakers out on to the terrace and turned the sound up to full volume. Diana and I sat side by side in the gathering twilight while the strains of Beethoven's Pastorale boomed out over the loch and re-echoed from the hill beyond.

It lifted us out of a mood of sadness that one part of our lives was coming to an end. But with everything which ends there is always a new beginning.